BIG CITIES AND MOUNTAIN VILLAGES

An expat's holiday in Italy

NOOR DE OLINAD

PREFACE

This travel memoir is a snapshot of Italy in 2006 and not intended as a practical travel guide. If I were to recount every detail of my trip, this would be a very long book. Instead, for your enjoyment and my sanity, I have cut out the boring bits and kept the most entertaining and touching moments, recreating events and dialogue from memory. Names of places were retained, but I changed names of mentioned individuals to protect their anonymity.

CHAPTER 1
ALL ROADS LEAD TO ROME

"**M**um, dad, I have something to tell you."

"Oh good, you're back in time for dinner," Mum said.

"Why did you work an extra shift?" Dad asked.

"I need the money. Anyway, I said I have something to tell you." The envelope in my hand grew damp with sweat. "Where's Marina? I'll tell you all together."

My younger sister strolled into the room cradling our well-fed cat. "Susu want tuna for dinner?" she cooed.

"Hurry up and sit down, the lasagna's growing cold," Mum said.

I waved the envelope over my head. "Hellloooo! I'm *trying* to make an announcement!"

Dad looked up from his plate and his eyes narrowed. "Is that another speeding fine? Or did you dent my car again? We really need to work on your parallel parking."

I rolled my eyes and sighed. "*That* was an accident. And this is much more important." I paused for dramatic effect. "I'm going to Italy."

My family looked at me blankly, then dad cleared his throat.

"Yes, we know you want to go. You keep telling us."

"No, no. I said I'm *going* to Italy. I booked my tickets today."

Mum gasped and dropped her fork. "You didn't!"

"Yeah, I did. But don't worry, I won't travel alone and stay in hostels. I've booked a tour."

"Aren't they expensive?" Marina asked.

"Well, um, it was a bit more expensive than I thought, but it will be worth it – this tour goes to Pompeii and not many do, you know. Anyway, don't worry, I've got it all worked out. I'm going to work some extra shifts and save more money."

"Soooo… you basically spent your life savings," Marina said exactly what I was hoping she wouldn't.

"Noor! You didn't, did you?" Mum demanded. "You've been working and saving since you were 14! What about university?"

"Relax mum, I've already paid for my uni books."

Dad frowned. "You're too young to travel alone. You're only 18!"

"That's why I booked a tour," I told him smugly. "I won't be alone. And you can't talk – you started globetrotting when you were 21."

"21 is not 18. I was more mature and the world was different then, it was safer."

My shoulders tensed. "Look, I have to do this *now*. Grandma's not getting any younger. What if she dies suddenly like great aunt Denise? And I haven't seen Uncle Francesco or our cousins since I was ten!"

Nobody said anything. The move to Australia had been difficult and for years money had been tight, so we hadn't even been able to return for great aunt Denise's funeral.

"I promised grandma I would go back," I told them, jutting my chin out, but no one argued.

"It's not one of those tours where all they do is get drunk, is it?" Dad asked.

A half smile twitched at my lips. "No."

Dad smoothed his moustache. "Well, since you're going we better do some shopping. I want to send some gifts to family and friends."

I slid into my seat and helped myself to a large slice of mum's mouth-watering lasagne. "Fine, but I need to save some room for souvenirs. I'm doing the tour before going up to stay with grandma. I'll spend Christmas with her and come back in February before uni starts. See? I've got it all worked out."

"Three months with an 84 year old woman, in a 500 year old house with no indoor toilet and only a woodstove to keep warm in winter? Are you sure you know what you're doing?"

"I've lived there before you know," I pointed out to dad. "I like the cold."

"She'll make you use the chamber pot like when we were little," Marina sniggered.

I cringed. "No way."

Mum and dad looked at each other and laughed.

"It will be a good experience for you," Dad said a little too smugly.

THE FOLLOWING months flew by and my excitement was dampened slightly by stress. My tour had been cancelled so the company moved me to one that started a day earlier – in the morning when my flight was scheduled to land. If my flight wasn't delayed and I rushed to the hotel, I might make it in time for the start of the tour. Otherwise I would have to join them the next day.

After a very long flight, I landed in Rome in the early hours. By the time my luggage turned up and I found my pre-booked taxi, I was sweating with anxiety. It was my lucky day though, because when I arrived at the hotel there was no sign of the tour bus. I thanked the taxi driver and rushed inside.

The man behind the reception desk smiled. "Good morning. How may I help you?"

"Buongiorno, ho una prenotazione. Ecco i miei documenti." *(Good morning, I have a reservation. Here are my documents)*

"You speak Italian wonderfully!" He answered in Italian.

I smiled. "I'm Italian."

"What part of Italy are you from?"

"Piemonte, but my family moved to Australia 8 years ago."

"Ah, si!" He nods his head a few times. "You speak Italian very well for someone who left so young. But you speak it with a bit of English accent."

Heat flooded my cheeks. Moving countries had taught me to speak in a sort of flat and even way to be better understood, making me sound very boring compared to the Italians' melodious speech patterns. At times I ended up sounding more British than Australian with my careful 'pronoun-ciation'.

"I'm looking for my tour group," I nudged my booking papers across the counter. "The tour is supposed to start today."

"Yes, they are leaving now." He pointed to a large bus that had appeared in the courtyard.

A tall man with a clipboard was directing the small crowd gathered onto the bus.

"Oh no! Wait!" I yelled, sprinted towards him. "Waaaait for meeeee!"

Everyone stopped what they were doing and turned to stare.

I stopped abruptly in front of the man with a clipboard, huffing and clutching my ribcage.

"You must be Noor," he said with a smile. "I did not think you would arrive in time. I am your tour guide, Marco."

"I just −" I gasped, trying to catch my breath. "- ah-arrived from the airport."

"Very lucky. If you come a few minutes later you would have missed the first day of tour."

I looked back towards the reception desk. My suitcase had

fallen down and my documents were still sitting on the counter. "I haven't finished checking in," I wheezed.

"Come, I help you check in. Leave suitcase at hotel, just take what you need for the day."

I nodded and followed him inside, my shoes sliding a little on the smooth marble floors.

"You get your things, I take care of this," Marco said and launched into rapid Italian with the man behind the reception desk.

I ripped off the plastic wrap around my suitcase and yanked out my winter coat.

Marco laughed. "Relax. Now you are here, I wait for you."

I smiled and double checked I had everything I needed for the day. "Thanks for waiting."

"You very welcome. Now, if you are ready we go."

I followed him onto the bus and flopped into the first empty seat I saw.

"Okay, here we go!" Marco's voice rang over the chatter. "I am Marco your tour guide, and this is Valerio our bus driver. Give him clap everybody."

He waited for our clapping to finish before continuing. "Today we drive around Rome and introduce you to the eternal city. While we drive there, I introduce you to each other. Here we have Mr and Mrs Johnson from South Africa. He is doctor so very good for us."

Polite laughter rippled through the bus.

Marco pointed his long finger to a couple. "This is Jack, Hilary and their little girl Tiffany all the way from USA! Tim and Mary from New Zealand, and we have lots and lots of Australians!"

My neck followed Marco's finger as he pointed out all the Australians on the bus and finished the introduction with the Malaysian family of five and couple from Singapore on their honeymoon.

The two Australian girls on tour seemed to be around my age and the rest were young children or middle aged people.

I smiled and leaned back in the chair. *It was silly to worry about travelling alone. Everyone seems nice and friendly.*

Marco turned off his microphone and sat down, only to jump up a second later.

"Ah! I almost forget!" He smacked his forehead. "I need you to tell me which excursions you want to do, and pay for them today so I can organize tickets. Remember, you only in Italy maybe once, so make most of it and see everything you can!"

I pulled out my travel documents and read over the list of excursions. A knot formed in my stomach. All the good excursions were optional with an additional charge. I pulled out my wallet and counted the notes and sighed. Marco made his way down the aisle, jotting down notes and taking money and stopped next to my seat.

"So, little Italian, how many excursions you want?"

"I – I'll go to the Sistine Chapel and the leaning tower of Pisa."

His eyebrows shot up almost into his perfectly combed back hair. "Only?"

"Yeah …"

"You don't want to go to museum of art in Florence? Or special dinner near Trevi fountain? You won't get to see Trevi fountain."

No chance I'm paying €50 for one dinner.

"I can do that after the tour," I said. "I'm staying in Italy for three months."

"Ah, lucky girl! Okay, so €36 for Sistine Chapel and €35 for Pisa."

I paid and waited for him to move on before counting what I had left. If I stuck to my meal budget of €20 a day, I would have enough money for gifts and hopefully wouldn't have to withdraw more from the bank. I had some money left in my account, but that was for emergencies only and once it was gone, so were my life savings.

I cringed but did not regret coming to Italy. I could always earn more money when I returned to Australia, but how many more times in my life would I be able to see my grandma and older relatives? Better to enjoy their company while I can.

THE REST of the day was spent hopping on and off the bus and trying not to get run over by the chaotic traffic in Rome.

"Okay, group." Marco waved his long arms. "This good spot to take picture of Colosseum. Get a sandwich if you hungry and after ten minute we go closer to Colosseum. If you want to go inside, is extra but I don recommend it. Line is too long and we need to keep moving. After this, we return to hotel where you rest and get ready for romantic dinner near Trevi fountain."

People had already crowded around the sandwich stall but I hung back.

"Hello, I'm Rita and this is my husband John and our youngest, Maria."

"Hi."

John leaned back against a post and unwrapped his sandwich. "You're Aussie too, right?"

I nodded and tried not to stare at the sandwich as it travelled to his mouth.

"Are you travelling alone?" he asked.

"Yep. I have family here though, so I'm on my own just for the tour."

"Us too!" Rita said. "Our parents are from Italy and this is our first time visiting."

"You look young to be travelling alone," John said. "How old are you?"

"18, but I turn 19 soon."

"You're only a few years older than our Maria." Rita caressed her daughter's black, curly hair. "She's a bit shy, so it will be nice for her to have some young company on this trip."

7

I smiled at the teenager who was half hiding behind her mother.

"Okay group," Marco called out. "Let's cross to see the Colosseum. You can take pictures with gladiators, not real ones – they are just men in costumes, but you usually pay a few euro. Some people like this, but please don't take too long. We need to keep moving."

The group started shuffling towards the street crossing.

"Are you going to the Trevi fountain dinner tonight?" Rita asked.

"No, too tired. I've been flying since yesterday and I just want to sleep."

"Okay, we'll see you on the bus tomorrow morning then."

"Yep, sounds good."

MARCO KEPT TRYING to move the group along but we had to wait for those that insisted on going inside the Colosseum and those who wanted their photo taken with middle aged men dressed in cheap looking gladiator costumes. By the time we left, it was late afternoon and I could barely keep my eyes open.

It didn't take long to find my room and the first thing I noticed was the little flashing red light on the phone. My family's familiar voices hit me with a wave of homesickness. It was a short message, checking that I had arrived safely and sending me their love. When the message ended, I pressed replay. It wasn't until the third replay that I noticed the tears on my cheeks.

Geez, I need to get a grip! I'm 18, in Rome and instead of exploring the city I'm in my room crying. Pathetic. It's not like I've moved here permanently! Some adventurer I turned out to be.

Pretending the tears had stopped flowing down my face, I had a shower and lay down for a quick nap before dinner.

The first chance I get, I'll buy a phone card to call them.

My stomach rumbling woke me several hours later. I

rolled over to look at the clock on the bedside table and cringed. It was too late and dark to walk to the city centre and I wasn't prepared to pay for a taxi. I would have to eat at the hotel's restaurant.

I better call grandma first and let her know I arrived safely.

Ring, ring.

"Pronto? (Hello?)"

"Nonna! It's me!"

"Ooooo! Noor, is it really you? Have you landed in Italy?"

"Yes, I arrived this morning. The tour started right away so I didn't have time to call you until now."

"I'm so relieved you arrived safely! When do you get here?"

I laughed. "Not for a couple of weeks, remember? We're leaving for Venice tomorrow."

"What a pity you won't have time to see my family there. Do you still remember my cousin Luigia?"

"Sort of, but I haven't seen any of our Veneto cousins for years."

"We'll call them together when you get here. Now pay attention. You need to be very careful while you are travelling. Especially in Rome."

"I know, I know. I already got that lecture from dad."

"Don't be cheeky. There are lots of pick-pockets that target tourists so you need to hide your money in your bra."

"What?!"

"Your bra, girl! Aren't you listening to me? Fold the money into a handkerchief, and tuck it into your bra. Only keep ten euros or so in your wallet in case it gets stolen."

I rolled my eyes. "Don't worry, I'm not going to get robbed. I bought a money belt that I can hide under my jumper."

"Oh miss smarty-pants, don't you think a professional pickpocket would know how to steal a money belt? All tourists wear those. No, the safest place is your bra. That way if anyone is trying to steal your money, you'll know."

"And just how am I supposed to take money out to pay for things if it's in my bra? Ha! Didn't think of that, did you?"

"You keep a little in your wallet, then go to the bathroom if you need to take more out."

"Hmpf." There was some logic in her argument, but I had no intention of abandoning the money belt I had bought just for this trip. "Is Uncle Francesco with you?"

"No, but I'll see him in the morning."

"I'll call him tomorrow from Venice if I get some time."

"He's picking you up from the airport in Milan."

"I know, dad told me."

"I've prepared your room."

"Thanks grandma."

"And I have a surprise for you."

"What is it?"

"I made your favourite - stuffed zucchini flowers from my garden. I froze them all for you and wouldn't let your uncle eat them."

I grinned. "Thanks grandma! You're the best!"

"You better sleep now, you're probably exhausted."

"What are you talking about? It's only 7.30! Besides, I haven't had dinner yet."

"But it's already late for dinner… Wait - you're not going out to eat at night in Rome are you? Not by yourself!"

"No, relax. The hotel has a restaurant. I'll eat something here."

"Don't go out at night by yourself."

"Okay, okay! Geez, you sound just like dad. I'm 18, you know!"

"So what? I'm 84. It's dangerous to go out at night. Promise me you will be careful?"

"Yes, I promise. Stop worrying, I can take care of myself."

"Hmpf. Go eat. And call me again soon or I will worry about you."

"I will, I promise. Goodnight grandma. I can't wait to see you!"

"Me too. I got everything ready for you here. Have fun."

"Love you, goodnight."

"Goodnight."

Smiling, I hung up, smoothed my hair, put on a pair of shoes and took the lift down to the reception desk.

"Scusi, dove` il ristorante?" *(Excuse me, where is the restaurant?)*

The young man pointed behind me. "It is there, next to lounge."

"Grazie."

I crossed the lobby and froze. A crystal chandelier was hanging above tables covered in white cloths. The silver cutlery glinted under the soft light and flowers decorated the tables. I gulped. I didn't need to look at the menu to know that one meal here could easily use up two days' worth of food money.

A young man was standing near the entrance. The black pants, vest and tie he wore contrasted with the crisp white of his shirt.

"Buonasera. Table for one or more?"

"One."

He nodded and waved his arm around the room. "We are quiet tonight. Choose anywhere you like."

"I only want a light meal, is that okay?"

"Of course. You can order anything you like. Come, this nice table. I light candle for you."

"It's okay, I don't need a –"

He finished lighting the candle and put a napkin over my lap before handing me the menu. "I make recommendations. Tonight, chef special is veal cutlets cooked in red wine. Or if you like seafood, chef make excellent lobster."

"Um… I'll have the grilled vegetable, please."

"Excuse? I do not hear, you talk too quietly."

Cheeks burning, I repeated my order a little louder.

"Yes, excellent choice for entree. And for main?"

"Just the vegetables please."

"Nothing else?!"

I shook my head.

"Are you sure? Is very little dish. Only enough for entree."

I plastered a smile on my face. "I'm on a diet."

He looked me up and down. "Why? You no need to."

Oh, geez! Why can't you just take the order and go? Now I have to keep lying about a fake diet!

"I'm going to stay with my grandmother for three months and I'm sure she'll fatten me up."

He laughed. "You must be Italian. Where are you from?"

"Piemonte."

"Ahhh, yes. Excellent food there. Very well, I bring you vegetables."

By the time he returned with the very small plate with some pieces of grilled vegetable on it, the complementary breadbasket on the table was empty. Without saying anything, he re-filled it and joined his colleagues.

Within 15 minutes, I was done and waving to get his attention.

"Can I bring you coffee or sweet?"

"Oh no, thank you. I'm full." I patted my stomach and smiled. "Can I have the bill?"

"We put it on your room tab. You pay when you check out of hotel."

"Okay, great. Thank you so much."

I stood up and hurried away. *Sistine chapel, leaning Tower of Pisa*, I told myself over and over. They had better be worth a skipped lunch and miserable dinner.

IT WAS WORTH IT. I looked up at the beautifully painted images until my neck hurt, and then I interlocked my fingers behind it so I could continue staring. Of all the treasures I saw in the Vatican, this was the most beautiful.

"We leave now," Marco whispered in my ear.

I frowned, eyes fixed on the image of God reaching out to Adam. "Already?"

"Is long drive to Venice and we need to leave now so we arrive for dinner. Wait for me outside door - is he taking more picture? I told him no!"

Rubbing the back of my neck, I headed for the exit where most of the group was already assembled. I listened to their chatter about how beautiful the Vatican was but didn't join in. The whole visit was rushed and besides the Sistine Chapel, I couldn't remember anything clearly. The whole morning was captured in my mind as flashes of gold and riches of former eras, the feel of cold marble and a hushed silence that saturates ancient buildings.

I hope the rest of the trip isn't rushed like this.

Marco herded us into a piazza outside of the Vatican to wait for our bus and assured us Valerio would be here in less than ten minutes. That was plenty of time for what I wanted to do.

"Marco, I'm going to make a quick call but I'll keep an eye out for Valerio."

"Sure, but don't go far."

I nodded and ran to the small store across the piazza, bought an international phone card and rushed to the phone booth before I lost my chance. Holding the receiver between my head and shoulder, I punched in the numbers and held my breath as it rang.

"Noor?"

"How did you know it was me?"

"Who else would it be at this time of night? Your mum is next to me. We waited up in case you called."

"Did you get there okay?" Mum asked.

"Yeah, everything went fine and they didn't lose my luggage."

"We called the hotel and left a message," Dad said.

"I know, I heard it but I couldn't call you because I didn't have the phone card. I made it in time for the start of the tour so I was out of the hotel all day."

"How is it?" Dad asked.

"Umm, not quite what I expected," I admitted, keeping an eye on Marco on the tour group. "It's very fast. We get off the bus, take some pictures and run back to the bus. I mean, we just got to Rome and we're already leaving for another city!"

"That's what bus tours are like," Dad said. "You'll spend more time on the freeway than actually seeing Italy."

"Dad, Mum - I have to go, the bus is here. I'll call you again tonight from Venice."

"We love you, and your sister says hi," Mum said.

"Be careful," Dad said.

"Love you, bye!" I put the receiver back and ran.

I GLANCED down at my watch and sighed.

"We've been driving for five and a half hours. I didn't realise Venice was so far," I said.

Maria smiled and nodded.

"So… have you been to Venice before?"

Maria shook her head.

"Me either but I've been to Veneto before, when I was very young. My grandmother is from this area. She still has family here. Do you have family here too?"

"Um, further down," Maria mumbled.

"Have you met them before?"

She shook her head.

"Well, I'm sure you'll have fun in Ital –"

"Buona sera everybody!" Marco's voice boomed throughout the bus. "Buona sera means good evening. We are almost at our hotel and you have free evening so you have to organize dinner for yourself. There is restaurant at hotel and some places near, but not many. Tomorrow morning we take small boat from mainland and cross the water to Venice. How much longer Valerio? Two minutes? Very good."

"Is he still talking to us, or has he forgotten the microphone is still on?" I whispered to Maria.

She shrugged and gave a small smile.

Valerio was pulling into a parking area and a bright light drew my attention. A very small corner shop, like a mini supermarket, was just down the road from the hotel and best of all, it was still open. Marco handed out room keys while Valerio unloaded our luggage and left them outside our rooms.

As soon as I had my key, I ran to the little shop on the corner.

"Scusi, siete ancora aperti?" *(Excuse me, are you still open?)*

"Si, prego," said the middle aged woman in a thick coat. *(Yes, come in.)*

I stepped inside and grinned. For a small shop, it had everything I could possibly need. Fresh bread rolls, a delicatessen section with cured meats, a fridge area with yogurts and milk, fresh fruit and vegetables, large water bottles and toiletries. I hauled a couple of packs of six water bottles up to the counter, chose a couple of bread rolls, some ham, fruit and the same type of snacks I used to eat as a child in Italy.

"Can I come back for the second water pack? I'm staying in the hotel just down the road."

"Yes, of course. Your Italian is very good. Where did you learn it?"

"My dad is Italian, and we used to live in Piemonte. My grandma is from this area, actually."

"Ah, you're technically a local." She smiled, crinkling the skin around her warm brown eyes.

I laughed. "Yeah, I guess I am a bit of a local. It's my first time to Venice though."

The woman nodded, packing my purchases in a couple of bags. "You will like it, it's beautiful. Are you sure you can carry these by yourself?"

"Yes, the hotel is close. I'll just drop these off in my room and come back. See you soon."

I hope I'm allowed to take food up to my room.

I shifted the pack of water bottles in my arms and walked through the lobby as quickly as I could, trying not to draw the hotel staff's attention. Balancing the water bottles on my knee, I fiddled with the key.

"What have you got there?"

"Huh?" I turned around. A middle aged couple was coming out of their room. "Hi, I'm Tim and this is the wife, Mary. You're one of the Aussies. We're from New Zealand."

"Nice to meet you." I nod my head at the shopping bags in my hand. "There's a small supermarket just down the road, so I bought a sandwich for dinner and stocked up on water. The prices are cheaper than larger stores."

"Just down the road?" Mary asked.

"Yeah, you can't miss it. I'm walking back for my second pack of water, I can take you with me if you like."

"Cheers, that would be great," Tim said.

I left my food and drink in the room and walked back to the shop with Tim and Mary. A few others from the tour were already there buying snacks and water. I thanked the woman behind the register and carried my water back to the hotel.

My sandwich was fresh and filling, I had enough snacks for a few days (in case I couldn't find more cheap places to eat), and enough water to last me most of the trip.

All of this for less than twenty euros! I grinned.

I was too tired to write in my travel diary for long, so after a quick shower I lay down on the firm mattress and fell asleep almost immediately.

CHAPTER 2
VENICE, THE CITY OF DREAMS

For the first time in my life, I woke up before the alarm clock rang and got ready quickly.

"Morning."

I turned around and waved, one finger keeping the lift doors open. "Good morning."

"You're one of the Australians, right?"

"Yes. I'm sorry, I don't remember your names?"

"I'm Hilary. This is my husband Jack and our daughter Tiffany."

"Nice to meet you. Are you getting the lift too?"

"Yeah, thanks."

"What part of America are you from?"

"New Jersey," Jack said, smoothing back his heavily gelled shoulder length black curls. "But my grandparents came from Italy, so I've brought the family for a holiday."

The elevator doors opened onto the lobby.

"Good morning," said Marco.

"Good morning" we echoed.

"The dining room is over there. If you need something, ask the waiter Lorenzo. I make quick phone call and join you."

I followed the family into the dining room. At one end

were a couple of tables pushed together with food arranged on top. The rest of the room was as shabbily decorated as my bedroom, but at least the furniture looked as sturdy as the day it was bought in the 1960s.

"I hope they have bacon," Jack said, grabbing a plate. "They didn't have bacon at the last hotel."

"They eat ham here, honey."

I walked up the food table and reached for a plate, my eyes darting to the tall waiter looking at me with narrowed eyes. When Jack placed five boiled eggs on his plate, Lorenzo the waiter made a tut-tut sound with his tongue. I quickly made a ham and cheese bread roll, picked up a yogurt and apple and moved away to find a seat when someone gasped.

I turned back towards the food tables. Lorenzo's hands flailed and strange gasping sounds came out of his mouth. Jack, completely ignoring him, piled a small mountain of sliced ham, bread, butter, fruits, cakes and every other kind of food on his plate.

"Noor, over here!"

I turned to see Rita waving from the back of the dining room. "Come join us."

I smiled and walked over, nodding hello to the group members along the way.

"I'm so excited to see Venice today!" said Rita.

"Me too," I said.

John chuckled. "That waiter doesn't look very happy."

We all turned to look. Lorenzo's face was an interesting shade of red, his eyes fixed on the full plate in Jacks' hands as he walked towards his family

"No! No!" he shouted with a heavy Italian accent. "You take too much!"

Jack looked over his shoulder. "What?"

"You take too much food! Not enough for everybody!"

Jack turns around slowly and looks up at Lorenzo with narrowed eyes.

The room falls silent. All eyes turn to the two men.

"*What* did you say?"

Lorenzo points a long finger at Jack's plate.

"*You*," he spits out, "take *too much*. Not enough for everybody."

"That's not my problem. The hotel knew how many people were coming, they should have prepared more food."

"We prepare enough!" Lorenzo shrieks. "You eat too much!"

I look around the room. People are staring, some with food halfway to their mouth. One man stands up and tries to calm them down but they ignore him.

Marco runs into the room.

"I'll call you back!" He yells into the phone and jumps between Jack and Lorenzo, holding them apart with his arms.

In a low and soothing voice, he calms them down enough so the shouting stops but Lorenzo storms off, his dark eyebrows pulled together, his lips pressed in a thin line.

Jack sits down with his family and people return to their breakfast.

The buffet table is not refilled.

AFTER A SHORT BUS DRIVE, we clambered onto the boat, trying not to fall overboard as it rocked from side to side in the choppy waters. I followed the others below deck to the seating area, but the noisy chatter and heat from so many bodies crammed together sent me scurrying back to the deck.

"Marco, can I stay up here?"

"Oh, but it is too cold!"

"I like the cold."

Marco shrugged elegantly. "Okay, I ask the captain. Luca, this girl is Italian and can speak well. She would like to stay up here. Can she?"

"Is rough water today. You won't be scared?"

I shook my head. "I've never been on a boat before, it seems very exciting."

Luca laughed. "All right but you must hold on or you will go overboard."

"Luca, is this your son Tommaso? He's so big now I almost didn't recognise him."

Tommaso smiled and waved. "Ciao Marco, it's been a while."

"So, you're a sailor like your father? That's great." He pointed to me. "Make sure she doesn't fall in the water or I will have to fill out a lot of paperwork."

Tommaso nodded and steered me to the steel railing that ran around the boat. "Hold tight here. Both hands."

Marco sighed. "I wish I can stay but I have to look after the others. Don't fall in!"

I laughed and gripped the railing tighter. "Don't worry, I won't let go."

With a cheerful wave, Marco disappeared below deck and Tommaso untied the boat from the wooden post.

"It is pity that we have fog, you won't see much," Luca said.

"I don't mind," I answered. "It's much better than being trapped downstairs like a sardine."

I thought I heard a laugh, but it was hard to tell with the loud sound of waves smacking against the sides of the boat.

For a while, we navigated the choppy waters in silence. It took all my concentration to keep my balance and stay upright.

"Want to steer?" Luca's voice boomed in my ear.

"What?!"

He laughed and motioned me forward with his hand.

"But... but... I don't know how! I don't even have a car license -"

"You don't want to?" Tommaso asked.

"Yes, but what if I hit one of those wooden pole things sticking out of the water?"

Tommaso grinned. "Don worry, we help you. Try, is fun."

Luca positioned me in front of the wheel and placed my

hands in the right position. "I will show you how. Now, hold steady and turn when I tell you."

My heart thumped, my eyes darting back to the wooden poles.

"Are you sure this is okay? I don't want to hit those and ruin your boat."

"You won't. They are bricole, they tell us where to go in the water."

Luca leaned against the railing and started humming.

I took a deep breath and clutched the wheel, holding it steady as ordered. A few uneventful minutes passed. My shoulders loosened and my grip relaxed. The air smelled like seaweed and every now and then a cold spray of water hit my face, but I couldn't stop grinning.

Luca put his hat on my head and chuckled. "Now you look like a sea captain! Tomaso, doesn't she look like a sailor now?"

Tommaso saluted and laughed. "Aye, captain!"

"Now turn the wheel left," Luca ordered.

I pushed the wheel to the left but it didn't move.

I pushed harder.

It didn't move.

"Turn!" Luca commanded.

"It's not turning!"

"Turn harder!" Luca's said sharply.

My head snapped up. A large wooden pole stuck out of the water and I was headed straight for it.

Sweat trickled down my spine. I gripped the wheel and turned as hard as I could.

'More! Turn more!" Luca shouted.

I stepped back, leaned on the wheel and used my body weight to turn it.

"Gnnnmmaaargh... " was the sound that came out of me.

Luca stepped behind me and grabbed the wheel, trapping my hands underneath his calloused ones. "Like this. Turn."

I bit my lip to stop myself crying out in pain as his hands crushed my fingers.

The wheel turned and the boat sailed past the pole.

Weak with relief, I leaned against the wheel and drew a deep breath.

"You make it look so easy."

Luca smiled. "Want to keep steering?"

"No thanks!"

Still tidying the ropes, Tommaso laughed.

I took off the captain's hat and held it out to Luca. "I'll be the lookout and watch for Venice."

"Oh, why? You were so good," Tommaso said.

"I almost crashed the boat! No, no. I don't think I have what it takes to be a sailor."

Luca and Tommaso laughed and let me retreat back to the safety of my rail.

"We are almost there," Luca told me. "Look through the fog."

I squinted at the blurry shapes behind the thick white fog.

Like a veil lifting, the mists parted and the proud and ancient city appeared in all its glory.

"Venice!" I squealed and my crewmates laughed.

Luca steered the boat into an empty spot between a row of boats and Tommaso secured it with a thick rope.

"Thank you for letting me steer," I said, shaking their hands. "And I'm sorry I almost crashed your boat."

Luca shook his head and smiled. "You are welcome."

Marco's head appeared at the top of the stairs from the lower deck. "This way everyone," he called out over his shoulder. "This way to Piazza San Marco. Like my name, hahaha!"

"Thanks again Luca and Tommaso," I waved. "Ciao."

"Enjoy Venice. Arrivederci!" Tommaso waved back.

. . .

THE PIAZZA WAS CROWDED with hundreds of tourists and pigeons. Between their noise and the sound of water hitting the sidewalk, it was hard to hear Marco's voice.

"Behind me is the beautiful Doge's palace. Isn't it beautiful? I tell you interesting story. See the red columns?"

We all nodded like attentive schoolchildren.

"Do you know why they are red?"

We all shook our heads in unison.

"Because that is where they hung the prisoners."

My eyebrows shot up. *An unexpected dark side to a magical city.*

"Very clever Doge, no? When people of Venice walk past, they see beautiful white columns, and then the red ones to remind what happens if they disobey the Doge." Smoothing his perfectly combed back hair, Marco turned and waved his arm. "Follow me around Piazza San Marco, and be careful of the gypsies. One will distract you asking for money while another steals your wallet."

We followed Marco, sticking close together and stopping often to take pictures of the beautiful clock tower, Saint Mark's Basilica, the Campanile and even the flocks of pigeons. We admired the Bridge of Sighs, which sounded very romantic until Marco told us it was named like that because prisoners would sigh when they looked at Venice for the last time before being imprisoned. Or executed.

Marco kept up a brisk pace and by the time I had taken a few blurry photos, he was waving people through a door. "Hurry, glassmaking show is starting."

The others were already seated on wooden benches, facing a large furnace with a crackling fire. The well-dressed young woman at the front greeted us in English and introduced the master glassmaker and his young apprentice. She told us a little of the history of glass making in Venice and explained some of the techniques. The master glassmaker started working. He mixed some colours and pulled out the boiling hot molten glass. Eyes wide, I watched him blow into a long metal pipe, twirl the blob of glass and shape it into a rearing stallion. He dipped it into a bucket of cold water and put it on the table for us to admire.

The young woman let us take some pictures and steered us through to the gift shop area where brilliantly coloured glass artefacts were displayed from ceiling to floor. I pulled out my wallet and counted. I had allocated more spending money for Venetian glass gifts than any other part of the trip, but the prices were higher than I expected. I chose the gifts carefully, something for each family member.

Marco let us take our time buying and after everyone had spent enough money, he took us outside. "If you are doing optional excursion, stay with me otherwise have fun exploring Venice. We meet again in afternoon. Our boat will pick us up at five o'clock from bridge … 5 o'clock! If you are late, boat leave and you stay in Venice."

"How do we find the bridge? Does it have a name?" someone asked.

"Yes but don't worry about name. Just turn left from Piazza San Marco and count the bridges. Okay, optional excursion people follow me!"

"Wait, which bridge?" I called out but Marco had already walked off, closely followed by most of the group.

"Excuse me," I asked the woman next to me, "which bridge are we supposed to meet at?"

"I think he said the third bridge, where we were dropped off."

"No mum, I think it was the fifth bridge," said the young woman next to her.

"Oh, really?" she looked at me and shrugged. "Sorry, I'm not sure which one. If you get there a bit before five, just look for the group members."

"Good idea, I'll do that. Thanks."

We nodded awkwardly at each other and went our separate ways.

. . .

WITHOUT LOOKING at the map in my pocket, I started walking. I wanted to see the real Venice - the streets where locals lived, shopped, worked and went about their daily lives with the constant sound of shifting waters. I crossed a few bridges, took pictures of the brightly coloured houses, turned into a lane with graffiti on the walls and got completely and wonderfully lost.

There was hardly anyone walking around and the few people that were, were all locals. Some ignored me, but others nodded their head and said 'Buongiorno'. I stopped to take photos of a row of houses with small boats tied by the front door. Standing on the bridge gave me a perfect camera shot.

"Sono bello?" *(Am I handsome?)*

I lowered the camera from my eye and looked around.

"Sono qui." *(Over here.)*

I looked down at the two men grinning and waving. One is a portly sixty or so year old man wearing a cap and a thick wool jumper. His friend is younger, half his size but dressed in a similar fashion and holding a hammer. More tools and building material are on the ground next to them.

"Scusi il disturbo, prendevo una foto." *(I'm sorry to have bothered you, I was taking a photo.)* I point to the row of houses with small boats bobbing in front of them.

"Ah, peccato," the older one says. "Pensavo prendevi una foto di me, bello come sono." *(What a shame. I thought you were taking a photo of me, since I'm so handsome.)*

Grinning, he strikes a pose pretending to be flexing his biceps.

I burst out laughing and hold up my camera in their direction. "Se permette, prendo una foto." *(If it's okay with you, I will take a photo.)*

They nod and wave at the camera with big smiles on their faces.

"Grazie, buona giornata." I wave goodbye. *(Thank you, have a good day.)*

"Piacere. Arrivederci!" *(Our pleasure. Goodbye.)*

I walked away chuckling. When I saw a small supermarket, I stopped to buy a sandwich which I ended up sharing with some pigeons who wouldn't leave me alone. I walked until my feet ached, then I sat down on the edge of a fountain and wrote in my travel diary. When they stopped throbbing, I walked some more and found a phone box. Completely forgetting the time difference, I woke my parents and spent the next couple of minutes apologizing and assuring them there was no emergency. I spent the next few minutes assuring grandma and Uncle Francesco that I was perfectly fine exploring Venice alone and that I would re-join my group soon. By the time I finished chatting, it was time to head back to Piazza San Marco.

The map showed me the general direction I needed to go in, but navigating the maze of small lanes in the inner part of Venice was more difficult than I anticipated.

The sky was growing darker.

Marco wouldn't really leave anyone behind in Venice, I told myself. *Would he?*

I tried to retrace my steps, but I had taken too many spontaneous turns. Without street signs or lane names, I couldn't find my location on the map so I asked the locals walking past for directions. Two hours and several wrong turns later, I burst out of the labyrinth.

The cold air smacked my sweaty, flushed face. I stood at the edge of the piazza with a hand over my thumping heart until I stopped panting.

Piazza San Marco was bathed in golden light. The sun had set, and the evening sky was a deep purple blue. I crossed the Piazza slowly, savouring the atmosphere and gentle stillness that had descended on the city.

Water slapped against the edge of the Piazza, thumping relentlessly. I walked down, counting the number of bridges and looking for the familiar faces of my group. There was no one at the fifth bridge, so I walked back to the first bridge and started again. There was no one at the third or fifth bridge, and no familiar face among the people walking by.

I chewed my bottom lip, pulling at the knots in my hair. *It must be one of the other bridges. I'll start again, and this time I'll stop at each one to check.*

The darkness was thickening so I listened for the sound of familiar voices and counted the number of bridges I crossed out loud, ignoring the looks from people walking by. I was back at the first bridge, heart thumping and sweating.

Don't panic! They have to be here somewhere. Worst case scenario, I catch a water taxi back to the mainland. Oh no ... what's the hotel name?

My stomach tightened.

What do I do? Should I walk down to the fifth bridge again?

I started jogging.

One, two – wait! Is that ...? It sounds like ...

A tall figure was waving a clipboard high over his head.

"This way!" he yelled to a few people rushing to board. "Is that everybody?"

He turned and placed a foot on the boat.

"Maaaarrcoooo," I shouted into the wind.

He paused and looked over his shoulder.

"Waiiiit for meeee!"

His eyebrows shot up, eyes wide, watching me race towards the boat.

I jerked to a stop in front of him and doubled over, gasping for breath.

"Ah, there you are. You look like a little lost bird."

"I was - " I gulped some air, "- afraid you would leave without me."

"I wouldn't do that!"

"But you said..."

Marco burst out laughing.

"No, no, no ..." he laughed some more. "I only say that to make tourists arrive on time."

"What?!" I resisted the urge to punch him in the face.

27

"Oh sorry. Did I scare you? I wouldn't leave without my tourists! I was just about to check if everyone was on board when I heard my name on the wind, like a ghost calling - Maaaarcooo."

He started chuckling and ushered me on board. I waved to Luca and Tommaso.

"Can I stay up here again?" I asked Luca. "I'd like to see Venice at night."

"Sure, but water is much rougher than this morning. You can't let go of the rail."

"I won't, I promise."

"Ah," Marco sighed. "You get to see Venice glittering in the dark and I have to go below to check on the others. My job is hard."

Luca rolled his eyes. "You see Venice lots of times. Go below so we can leave."

Chuckling, Marco held up his hands and joined the others below deck.

I watched Venice get smaller and smaller until it disappeared out of sight. Against the deep black of the sky, the distant lights in the ancient city seemed like twinkling stars on the horizon.

I'll come back, I promised myself. *I'll come back for the Carnevale and wear a beautiful mask and a renaissance gown.*

CHAPTER 3

THE CITY OF LOVERS, THE
CAPITAL OF ART

R ita's head popped up from the seat in front.
"How are you girls going?"

I plastered a smile on my face. "Fine."

"It's so nice that Maria has company her age."

"Soooooo, here we are!" Marco's voice boomed through the bus.

I sighed in relief. The whole bus ride had been one long complaining session about how annoying her older siblings were, and how boring high school was.

"You all know the famous story of Romeo and Juliet so I won't tell you again. But what you don't know, is that Verona has many Roman ruins. We will see some before going to Juliet's house. Unfortunately we cannot go on the balcony because they are doing some work, but you can take picture with the statue of Juliet. Valerio will pull over here, so we must get off quick. Ready? Go!"

I grabbed my backpack and merged with the stampede rushing off the bus.

"Everyone here?" Marco counted heads. "Okay, good. Follow me, and stick close together."

Marco walked briskly, stopping for only a few minutes at various Roman ruins to explain some of the city's history before heading towards Juliet's house. The entrance was crowded with young couples exchanging passionate kisses or writing notes to Juliet and sticking them on the walls. The courtyard was just as crowded with tourists and young couples posing for a photo with Juliet's statue and buying love tokens.

Marco stood in the corner of the courtyard and waved his arms. "Come closer everyone. We line up here to take photo with statue. See how right breast is shinier than other? They say if you rub Juliet's breast, you have good luck in your love, so honeymoon couple – make sure you rub."

Chuckling, people turned to look at the blushing young Singaporean couple.

"Give me your cameras everyone, and I will take photo for you," said Marco.

I lined up for a photo but left poor Juliet's body alone. She had been bothered by tourists more than enough over the years. When the others went to buy love tokens from the gift shop, I went to read the notes and graffiti people had written on the entrance walls in many different languages. Love is clearly a universal desire.

A hand tapped my shoulder, jolting me out of my thoughts.

"There you are," said Marco. "We need to go back to bus now."

"Already?"

"Yes, it's a long drive to Florence and we need to stop to give breaks."

I nodded and glumly followed the others onto the bus.

VALERIO TURNED the bus down a driveway, flanked by a garden with large white globes that gave the lawn statues an otherworldly glow. He stopped in front of a multi-story, cream coloured villa and began unloading suitcases. After several minutes trying to find our suitcases in the dark, we

30

followed Marco to the reception desk and received our room keys.

I looked down at my suitcase and pack of six, large water bottles and sighed.

Just my luck to be on the second floor.

The lift was slow and the line to use it was too long, so I grabbed my suitcase and heaved it up the first flight of stairs then went back for my pack of six large water bottles. I dragged the suitcase up the second flight of stairs, went back for my water supply and couldn't find my room. Leaving them in a corner, I jogged down to reception and found out I was in the wrong section of the hotel. The line in front of the lifts had only reduced by a fraction so I started the process all over again, but this time I looked for my room first.

Huffing and sweating, I yanked my suitcase over the last step and stopped to catch my breath. The door on my right was open and a middle aged man stepped out.

"Hello, you are on our tour."

"Yes," I puffed.

"I am Firash, and this is my wife and sons." He waved his arm at the four faces behind him. "We are from Malaysia."

"Nice to meet you," I wheezed.

"You are from Australia or America?"

"Australia."

"Traveling alone? You look young."

"I'm almost 19, and I have family in Italy."

"Ah, that is good. Are you on this floor too?"

"No, next one. I just stopped to rest before I go get my water. I accidentally went to the wrong part of the hotel before..." I chuckled weakly.

He chuckled. "Yes, I saw you take them on and off bus. Where did you get them?"

I told him about my supermarket shopping spree in Venice and how much cheaper it was than buying bottles from street vendors and restaurants.

"Very good. You good with money." He turned to nod at a teenage boy. "Aqil, learn from her and stop wasting money."

Aqil mumbled something incomprehensible.

"Well, I better get going. Nice to meet you, goodnight."

"Aqil will help you carry water."

"What? No, that's okay – I can manage."

"No, no. You are girl and he is strong boy. He carry it for you. Aqil, go."

"Really, I can manage –"

"It's okay, it's no trouble," Aqil smiled and pushed his glasses back up.

"If you need something, you come to us," the father ordered.

"Um, okay … thanks."

My muscles were trembling slightly from fatigue, and since Aqil had agreed, it seemed stupid to refuse help.

"Thanks Aqil," I said, walking down the stairs. "You really don't have to do this though. I can carry it by myself and you can tell your dad you did it."

"Nah, it's okay. I don't mind and it gives me a bit of freedom from my brothers."

I laughed. "Are you the oldest?"

"Yeah. They're still young and want to follow me everywhere."

"How old are you?"

"14."

I grabbed my suitcase where I had left it and led the way down the dimly lit corridor.

"This is my room. Thank you so much for your help."

"You're welcome. Goodnight."

"Goodnight, and thanks again!" I said to his retreating back, unlocking the door.

I switched on the light and gasped.

"*This* is my room?" I asked the vast, empty space.

I walked across the white tiled sitting room and climbed the small step into the sleeping area. The view from the window were the other windows of the U shaped part of the hotel, but I wasn't complaining. The mattress was comfortable and instead of a wardrobe I had an antique looking large dresser next to a wooden door that wouldn't open. I walked back across the sitting room into the similarly white tiled bathroom with an enormous walk in shower.

"Wow!" I breathed, sinking into one of the small black couches.

I ran my fingers across the softness of the material.

Is this leather? Who cares? It's comfortable, and the TV screen is so big!

Grinning, I unpacked for the night, showered and climbed into bed. My eyes closed and my breathing deepened.

Creak.

I rolled over and pulled the blankets up higher.

Rattle, rattle.

My eyes flew open.

What was that?

I strained my ears. A few seconds later, the sound came again.

It sounds like a doorknob turning. It's too close to be the front door.

Sitting up, I switched on the night light, shoved my glasses on and stared at the only other door in my room.

I must have been dreaming.

The doorknob turned.

Gasping, I jumped out of bed.

The doorknob turned again, got jammed and rattled the way when someone tries to force something open.

Leaping to the large dresser, I pushed it across the door and jumped back.

I stared at it, completely still and silent.

My eyelids grew heavy and I started shivering. Retreating under the covers, I kept the light on and watched the door until everything went black.

· · ·

I woke up before my alarm clock rang with dark circles under my eyes and got ready in record time. I didn't really believe in ghosts, but rattling doorknobs was making me rethink about supernatural beings. Stumbling out the door, I rushed to lock it and dropped the key. That's when I noticed a door next to mine. I stared at the number of my neighbour's room, blushing and cringing.

Ghosts! I mentally smacked myself. *Damn, I didn't even notice it last night! It must be joined to my room. Hahaha, ghosts…*

Relieved my room wasn't haunted, I yawned through breakfast and didn't relax completely until we were away from the hotel, walking in the mild winter sunshine.

Marco led the way, enthusiastically waving his arms and pointing out one beautiful sight after another. I admired the architecture of the Palazzo Vecchio (also known as Palazzo della Signoria), and Palazzo Uffizi. I stared in disbelief at the realistic detail of the life like statues displayed in the Piazza della Signoria. The historical centre was fascinating but nothing, absolutely nothing, compared to the timeless elegance of Brunelleschi's Duomo reaching to the heavens and breathtaking Gates of Paradise on the Baptistery. Half a day was not enough time to begin appreciating the beauty of Florence. I could spend an entire week visiting old palaces and art galleries, but for now I would enjoy some free time walking around the city while the others went on the optional excursion of the Galleria dell' Accademia.

"Hi, I'm Jessica."

I turned to look at the speaker, a slim girl around my age with ginger hair and almost translucent skin. I had seen on her the bus, but this was the first time she had talked to me.

"Hi, I'm Noor."

"Are you going to the art gallery?"

"No, I'm just going to walk around."

"Me too. These optional excursions are too expensive. Do you mind if I walk with you?"

I smiled. "Not at all."

Maria was with her parents and I felt safer walking with others instead of alone. Jessica wasn't very talkative, but I didn't mind. We took pictures for each other and looked at the beautiful architecture that surrounded us in every direction.

"I love the coffee here. Do you mind if we stop at a café`?" Jessica asked.

"Sure. I don't drink coffee but I can wait for you."

"I heard you speaking Italian to Marco. You seem fluent."

"Yea, I'm half Italian and used to live in the country."

"Wow, that's so cool! Hey, could you order for me? My Italian is really bad."

"Yeah, no problem."

I walked into the café with her and translated, explaining that she would have to drink it standing up outside or pay extra to sit down inside. While she enjoyed her coffee, a few others from the tour group joined us and having heard on the grapevine that I could speak Italian, they asked for help ordering coffee and ice-cream.

I hope they don't make a habit of this, I thought, lining up to order. *I can't really refuse because then I would seem rude, but if the only time they talk to me is to order stuff for them… Maybe I shouldn't have spoken so much Italian.*

BY THE TIME THEY FINISHED, Marco was waiting at the designated meet up spot with the rest of the group and hurried us onto the bus. Jessica went to her usual seat and I sat next to Maria who chatted about the souvenirs she bought. It wasn't long before Valerio pulled into a large, empty car park with a bright red and yellow smaller version of a steam train.

"Okay everybody," Marco called out from the front of the bus. "We swap our bus for a train! Fun, no?"

"That?! I'll never fit in that. It's for children!"

I turned my head to look at Tim's tall frame crammed in the bus seat and silently agreed with him.

"No, no." Marco waved his hands. "It looks small but is plenty of room. And is only way into Pisa."

The train compartment was quite comfortable for me, and others of my average height. The rest had to origami themselves in while the group laughed at their efforts.

"I hope this is safe," I chuckled. "It looks like it's made out of plastic."

The honeymoon couple were too busy taking a couple photo to reply.

With everyone on board, the train took off with a Chooo-chooo sound. It was surprisingly faster than I expected and every time it swerved, I clung onto the seat and hoped the train wouldn't turn over. Getting out of the compartments, particularly for the tall people, resembled clowns getting out of a miniature car.

"Signori, I give you leaning tower of Pisa!" Marco flung out his arm.

I looked behind him at the intricately ornate row of creamy white buildings.

"This is Campo dei Miracoli, Field of Miracles, and there are three very important buildings. First is the Baptistery, then Duomo and then the famous leaning tower," said Marco. "We cannot go inside anymore, but if you stand in this spot –" he moved a few steps to the right, "you can take photo like you holding tower up. Like this."

He flexed an arm and pretended to push the tower with the other. I laughed with the others and lined up for my turn to have a photo taken. Marco patiently took photo after photo until everyone was satisfied.

"Okay everyone, we go now," Marco announced.

"Do we have time to go to the bathroom first?" Rita asked.

"Yes, of course. Over here. Men on left, women on right but you must pay €1 to use them."

"What?" Jack demanded. "Pay to use a toilet? That's ridiculous."

Marco shrugged. "Is something we do in Italy. It gives people work and pays to keep toilets clean for tourists."

I fumbled around my wallet for a coin and lined up with many of the others. The older woman sitting outside the toilet block was scowling, possibly because of the stench of urine coming from inside. Grimacing, I pulled up my scarf to cover my nose and dashed in and out.

THE EVENING PASSED BY PEACEFULLY, talking to my family and writing in my journal. My bags were packed and the alarm was set for the morning. After checking one last time the door in my bedroom was still locked, with the dresser in front of it, I got under the covers and left the night lamp on. My eyes closed, with images of beautiful Florence dancing behind my eyelids as I drifted to sleep.

CHAPTER 4
SAINTS AND SEAWEED

Valerio stopped the bus at the bottom of the medieval hill town of Assisi and we made our way up to St Francis' Basilica by foot. Hundreds of pilgrims filled the courtyard, with many more praying quietly inside. Even though I'm not a devout Catholic, I lit a candle to honour St Francis. As the patron saint of animals and the environment, he shared my love for flora and fauna and a guy like that definitely deserved a candle.

Marco gave us an hour to enjoy the exquisitely detailed architecture inside the church, and the mild sunshine bathing the life sized preseppio (nativity scene), outside on the lawn.

BACK ON THE BUS, I braced myself for the five hour drive to the Amalfi coast. For entertainment, Marco put on a documentary about the last days of Pompeii to enlighten us before our visit tomorrow. We stopped for food at Autogrill, one of the many highway rest stops we had seen as we drove around Italy. The cafeteria offered a variety of cooked food and sandwiches at a reasonable price, and the small supermarket section had many of my favourite childhood snacks. I ate my lunch in between helping several people order food, used the reasonably clean bathroom, stocked up on bottled water and snacks, and rushed back to the bus.

Squeezing past Maria, I flopped into the seat. She was scribbling in her diary so I looked out the window, fiddling with the zipper on my coat and thinking about lunch. Most of the people who had asked me to translate had never spoken to me before. Not even a hello when we all have breakfast together. Pushing my irritation away, I leaned back in the chair for a nap.

"Aaaaaaveeee Maaarriiiiiaaaaaaaa."

My eyes flew open. I leaned forward and looked around the bus.

Marco stood at the front, conducting the music blaring from the sound system with his microphone and a wicked grin. "A prayer so we reach the hotel safely."

I looked out the window and gasped. Our large bus was cruising along a twisty, windy road with only a small barrier between us and the cliffside. Waves crashed against the rocks below.

The bus turned a corner and I clutched the edges of my seat.

"Aaaaveeee Maaaariiiiaaaaaaaa!" Marco belted along with Andrea Bocelli.

I looked around. No one was smiling.

Marco stopped singing. "Ooooo! Why you all look so scared? Don't worry, Valerio has driven this road many, many times!"

He stopped the music. "Is okay, we won't fall into sea. Look out window; look at beautiful houses and lemon trees. Here they make the best limoncello."

Slightly calmer, I kept my eyes fixed on the colourful arrangement of yellow, white, red and pink houses built onto the Cliffside until we reached the hotel.

The sound of waves crashing against the shore boomed

loudly in my aqua and mint green decorated room. I was on the lower levels, closer to the water, and for some reason the bathroom smelled slightly of seaweed. I unpacked, and joined the others for the tour-included dinner.

DINNER WAS OVER and several people were already headed to their rooms, exhausted after spending most of the day on the bus. I walked across the dining room and waited for Marco to finish talking to the honeymoon couple. When they left, he looked at me and smiled.

"Are you looking forward to Pompeii tomorrow?"

"Yes," I answered, "but I actually wanted to ask about the night market. I'd really like to see it, but I can't find anyone else who wants to go. Is it safe for me to go alone?"

"Ah, what a pity. I thought more people would be interested." He smoothed his perfectly combed hair. "Yes, I think is safe."

"Is it worth the trouble to see it?"

"Oh yes! They have beautiful handmade things you only find in Amalfi. None of your friends want to go too?"

I shook my head. I had asked Rita and her family but they wanted to rest, and I didn't know anyone else well enough to ask them for their company.

Marco steered me to the reception desk and introduced me to Maria.

"I'd really like to go, but is it safe for me to go alone?" I asked in Italian.

Her large dark brown eyes crinkled as she smiled. "Of course. I walk home every night after work, sometimes very late, and I have never had a problem."

I grinned. "I was hoping you would say that. Is it easy to find?"

She nodded, making her dark curls bounce. "Turn right outside of hotel and walk straight until you reach the tunnel.

Go through the tunnel, and on the other side there is staircase that goes down to the beach and market."

"Grazie!"

"Have fun," Marco waved goodbye.

I waved back and left the lobby.

A SLIGHT BREEZE carried the scent of the sea to my nose. My only company were the stars above and the sound of waves crashing against the cliffside below. Smiling, I strolled towards the tunnel entrance.

On the left side of the tunnel, a man with short grey hair walked towards my direction. He glanced up, his hands shoved into the deep pockets of his long coat.

Humming Jingle bells under my breath, I walked on the right side of the tunnel.

His eyes darted towards me, then straight in front of him again.

I hope I can find something nice to take back for mum and dad. What the -!!

My knees jerked as my body jumped back a step.

The man had crossed to my side of the tunnel and was walking straight towards me, staring.

Maybe his house is on this side of the street.

I turned my back to the wall, giving him room to pass.

He moved straight at me.

I narrowed my eyes, my hands clenching into fists in front of my torso.

He paused for a second in front of me and kept walking.

I watched him walk away until he was out of sight.

Taking a deep breath, I leaned against the wall and wiped the cold sweat from my forehead. My knees were shaking. I looked at the tunnel entrance and chewed my bottom lip. It was probably my imagination, but it seemed much longer and more sinister than a few moments ago.

The market was so close, just on the other side of the tunnel. This could be my only visit to the Amalfi coast, but my feet refused to go back into the tunnel.

Sighing, I jogged back to the hotel and went to bed but it took a while before I could sleep.

CHAPTER 5

THE MASS GRAVE THAT IS
POMPEII

L ike every other morning, Marco stood by the bus door
greeting everyone.

"Good morning Marco."

"Ah, Noor, how was the market?"

"Oh, um … I didn't end up going."

He raised his eyebrows. "No? But you seemed so excited.
What happened?"

I cringed. *I can't tell him I ran back like a scared little girl.*

"I, um, got lost …"

"What a pity! Is ok, you see it next time and today you see
beautiful Sorrento."

Nodding, I gave him a weak smile and found my seat next
to Maria.

THE MORNING'S excursion focused on touring an inlaid wood
workshop and spending time in their gift shop. By the time
we finished, it was almost lunchtime but all the restaurants
were closed and grey clouds hovered ominously above.
Marco ushered us onto the bus for the half hour drive to
Pompeii, promising a decent and affordable meal when we
got there.

The meal was a sandwich from a snack bar near the entrance while we waited for the local tour guide to arrive. Four people who looked similar enough to be a family stood under a small marquee set up right outside the entrance gate. Their dark eyes followed us as we crossed the road and the two young men stepped in front of Marco, blocking his path.

Looking past Marco, the tall one flicked his cigarette ash on the ground and pointed to the tables behind him. "You want water? Only €5."

My jaw dropped. €5 for a small bottle of water?! Not even restaurants charged that much!

"Cheap souvenirs," the other called out. "Handmade in Italy."

"No thank you," Marco told them in Italian. "We don't have time."

It was too late. The brothers had lured several people towards the older couple by the tables.

"Handmade Cameo necklace," the dumpy middle aged woman called.

My eyes flicked to the table and the next second she stood in front of me.

"This real cameo necklace," she said in heavily accented English.

"Ah, this girl is Italian and can speak it very well," Marco told her.

Leaning down, he whispered. "Don't buy from them, everything is overpriced and fake."

I nodded and started to walk away. Quick as a flash, she snatched the necklace off the table jumped in front of me.

"So you Italian? What a pretty girl you are," she said dangling the necklace under my nose.

"Where you from?"

I stepped to the side but she blocked my path again. "Excuse me, I need to go."

"Don't tell the others, but I give you special discount because you are Italian."

"No thank you. I'm not looking for souvenirs."

"Look at necklace! Is beeeauuutiful and only €70."

"No thanks." Keeping my eyes firmly ahead, I moved around her and walked off.

She followed me. "Buy it as gift for your mother. She will love it."

I shook my head and kept walking but she cut me off again.

Marco walked up to us with a frown. "Everything okay Noor?"

"Yeah, thanks. I'm fine."

He nodded and rushed off to rescue someone who was cornered by one of the burly sons.

Clenching the necklace in her fist, the woman shoved it in front of my face.

"You know how much this cost in Florence? €70 is bargain. Real cameo!"

My mouth opened a closed a few times. "But I can see the glue! I *know* it's not real."

"Okay, I will give you a discount because you're Italian. €50."

I shook my head in disbelief. "*No*. I don't want it."

"Okay, 45."

"I can *see the glue*! Cameos are carved, not glued on!"

"Think of how expensive this is in Florence. €45 is great bargain."

I turned my back and walked away, but she followed right up to the entrance.

"Why you not buy?" She demanded.

I frowned at her. "It's fake and too expensive."

The local tour guide had arrived and was chatting to Marco. A few people walked up to them with a stunned expression, wearing new hats or carrying water bottles.

"It was the only way to get rid of them!" A woman muttered.

At that moment, the heavens opened and it started to

pour.

One of the brothers grabbed a bunch of umbrellas from the table and waved them in the air.

"€30 for umbrellas!"

"What?!" Jack yelled. "Two minutes ago it was 15!"

The other brother drew a puff from his cigarette and shrugged. "It was not raining two minutes ago."

Marco shook his head, his friendly smile gone. He marched up to them and spoke in rapid Italian. "Your behaviour is shameful! You're giving a bad impression of Italian people!"

I looked down at my soaking wet coat. *Damn! I should have bought a waterproof one.*

"€30 for umbrellas! Quick, before the price goes up!"

Grumbling and muttering, most of the group rushed to the tables to buy an umbrella. The others pulled out neatly folded rain coats from their pockets and slipped them on.

"You're not buying an umbrella?" Rita asked me.

"What's the point? I'm already soaked."

The middle aged woman was still hovering near me, clutching the necklace in her fist. "€35." She pressed her lips together and glared. "I have given you great discount!"

I frowned at her. *Is she going to follow me into Pompeii?*

"No."

"Is only €35! Buy it as a gift."

No wonder the others bought something just to get rid of them!

I rolled my eyes. "I'm not paying more than 15."

"No, it is too low."

I shrugged and turned my back to her.

She grumbled and muttered something that sounded like curses under her breath.

"Fine! 15 but you are robbing me!" she snapped.

Lips pressed together, I handed over the money and completely ignored her attempts to sell me an umbrella. Thankfully, she didn't follow me through the entrance.

"Well done!" Marco grinned at me. "I can't believe you bargained her down from €70 to 15! I go introduce guide."

THE SHORT WOMAN huddled under the umbrella adjusted her glasses and smiled.

"Everyone, this is Lucia and she will be local guide to Pompeii. Stay with her and don't get lost here, because once they close the gates you will sleep here tonight with the ghosts. Hahahah… okay, well enjoy and I see you at the front."

"Welcome everyone, first to Italy and now to Pompeii. This was a beautiful, thriving city with thousands of people. You get an idea of this from the big amphitheatre behind me. Is bad weather today, so I try not to keep you in rain for too long. This way, please."

The rain intensified. We walked slowly to avoid slipping on the paved street and in one place, we had to jump over a small river of water flowing in the middle of the street.

"Look down here," Lucia pointed to the ground. "You know what this symbol is?"

Jack leaned closer. "A stone penis?"

My eyebrows shot up.

Lucia nodded. "It is engraved onto the road to give visitors direction to the Lupanare. That is what they call brothel. We will go inside and see. Each room has a very well preserved mosaic to show what the prostitute's speciality is, or maybe even to teach inexperienced customers."

Only a few people could fit at a time. It was dark and very cramped. The rooms were tiny with small stone beds and no doors. Above each room was a beautifully made mosaic of happy looking women performing sexual acts, but I doubted the prostitutes forced to work here had been very happy.

We splashed through the torrential rain to look at the ruins of market shops, houses and exquisite villas. Everything had been destroyed by the volcanic eruption, but a lost city is not as tragic as the lost lives. Casts of some of the bodies found were displayed in glass cases, frozen in suspended motion, some with a terrified look on their face. One looked like it was sleeping. Others were the small bodies of children and dogs.

Death reigned here. It was a powerful reminder of the fragility of human life.

I DRAPED my drenched coat over a chair right under the heating vent and got under the blanket, waiting for my family to call. Pompeii had been a shock. It's not an archaeological ruin, it's a mass grave. I had never really thought about death before. I was only eighteen, and felt like I had all the time in the world but the people of Pompeii had lost everything so quickly.

Ring-ring.

I snatched up the phone.

"Mum? Dad? I love you!"

"How much money do you need?" Dad asked.

I rolled my eyes. "Nothing. I just miss everyone, that's all. How's Susu? Are you taking good care of her?"

"I fed her smoked salmon today," Marina chimed in.

Grinning, I leaned back on the pillows and listened to them trying to talk over each other.

CHAPTER 6
CAPRI

The van took a sharp left, flattening me against the window. Maria's bulk took up most of the two small seats so every time the driver turned or drove over a speed bump, her limbs knocked into me. The pungent odour of sweat from too many bodies in a small space was making my stomach heave.

"We're here!" Marco beamed. "Get your ferry ticket from me as you get off the van."

Finally! Fresh air!

Stuck by the window, I waited for everyone else to pass by and stumbled off the van.

Marco held out my ticket and smiled. "It's hard to believe it's a winter day, no? A little like Australian winter? Must be so nice."

I laughed. "It's not sunny and warm all the time in Melbourne, you know. It gets cold in winter, but no snow."

He nodded his head toward the ferries and started walking. "You miss snow?"

I slipped the ticket into my jeans pocket and took two steps to match one of his larger strides.

"Yeah. Besides family and friends, it's what I miss most. Mountains and snow."

"What about the food?"

"The only things I can't find are regional cheeses, but pretty much everything else is available at speciality supermarkets and delicatessens. There's a lot of Italians in Melbourne."

Marco's eyes widened. "Wow, sounds amazing!"

I nodded, carefully stepping onto the ferry.

"I have reserved the seats on top for the group," Marco pointed to a step ladder. "It has amazing view of Capri and Amalfi coast, but you can get a little wet from water splash."

A young man stepped in front of me and held out his hand.

"Tickets," he said softly, his vivid green eyes staring into mine.

"Oh, right. Sorry–" A little unnerved by his intense gaze, I pulled out the ticket and almost dropped it. "Sorry! Here it is."

Marco held out his ticket. "Most of the group will be up on the top deck to enjoy the view. You might get splashed by some water though."

The young sailor stamped our tickets and stepped aside.

"Come, let's see if we can find you a seat."

I followed Marco up the stair ladder but the top deck was already full. A little disappointed, I climbed down and walked into the covered seating area hoping to find a familiar face. The ferry lurched and my stomach rolled with it. I hurried into the closest empty seat and watched the shoreline slowly disappear from view, my arms wrapped around my stomach.

Did I eat something off at breakfast? I chewed my bottom lip. *All I had was an apple, yogurt and a muffin –*

The back of my neck prickled, giving me an eerie feeling of being watched. I turned around. The young sailor was standing in the middle of the lounge, arms crossed over his chest and his gaze fixed on me. Unabashed at being caught staring, he uncrossed his arms and sauntered over.

I moved to stand. "I'm sorry, is this seat reserved? I was feeling a little sick so I sat -"

"You can sit where you like."

"Okay, thanks."

"I heard you speaking Italian. Is this your first time on a boat?" he asked in Italian.

"No, I crossed to Venice from the mainland on a ferry."

He nodded. "You are a little sea sick. It will pass."

"But I didn't get sea sick crossing to Venice."

"Is different. This is open water. Much rougher."

I nodded but wasn't sure what he was talking about.

"Where are you from? How do you speak Italian but you are with tour group?"

I explained my background which led to the usual questions about my unusual name, what life was like in Australia and what I had seen so far in Italy.

"Do you like it here?" he asked.

"Yes, it's beautiful."

"You are also beautiful."

Heat crept up my face and flooded my cheeks. "Thanks."

I bet you say that to all the girls.

"How long are you here for? You're so beautiful! I want to see you again."

My eyebrows shot up. *Wow, this is such a cliché movie scenario. Does he really think I'm going to fall for that?*

"I'm leaving this afternoon."

"No! What a shame! I really want to see you again."

I shrugged.

"I have to go prepare to disembark. I'll see you again."

He walked away, glancing back over his shoulder several times.

Chuckling, I shook my head. As flattering as it was to be admired by a handsome sailor, I was too cynical to fall for his flattery.

I focused on my breathing to ease the sea sickness until we docked a few minutes later. Disembarking was almost as bad as the journey. Everyone wanted to get off at the same time and my body got swept along the crowd. The sailor with green eyes appeared in front of me.

What the?! How did he get through the crowd so quick?

"Bellissima," he said. "I will see you again."

I spotted Marco on shore waving his clipboard and group members making their way over.

"I have to go. Nice to meet you. Bye."

I pushed my way through the crowd and stumbled onto solid ground.

Marco was smirking at me.

"What?"

He pointed behind me.

I looked back. The sailor was waving his arms and yelling something as the ferry slid back into the sea.

"So you made a friend," Marco teased.

I rolled my eyes. "He wanted to know about Australia."

Marco chuckled and waved his arms to get the group's attention and explained the itinerary – a visit to a perfumery followed by an optional excursion or free time until we left by ferry for Rome, where Valerio would meet us with the tour bus and our luggage.

The whole of Capri seemed to be a giant hill with narrow, paved streets. It was a steep climb to the perfumery, but worth the effort. All the perfumes were made on Capri, using flowers grown on the Island. I took my time choosing a scent I thought mum would like to add to her already large perfume collection.

Marco, and most of the husbands on tour, waited patiently outside while the shoppers paid. I wrapped my scarf into a tight cocoon around the glass bottle and gently placed it in my bag. The perfume came in a box, but I wasn't taking any chances. Not for €30 for a small bottle.

"So," Marco beamed at the group, "now we continue to optional excursion of Capri with delicious sea food lunch by the sea. They catch it fresh this morning." He kissed his finger tips with a loud smack.

"What about those who aren't doing the optional excursion?" A woman asked.

"Ah, yes. I would recommend Tony's Pizzeria – they make real Italian pizza, very thin crust. Walk around Capri, enjoy the view and relax. Please don't be late and meet us same place we arrived by four. Have fun! Optional group, follow me."

As usual, Maria and her family were doing the optional excursion so I picked a random direction and turned to walk.

"Hi," a familiar voice said.

I looked back. "Oh, hi Jessica."

"You're not doing the optional excursion either?"

"No. I haven't done most of them."

"Yeah, me either. Too expensive."

I nodded.

"So, do you want to explore Capri together? We could try to find that pizzeria Marco was talking about and split the lunch bill."

I hesitated for a second. *You just want me to translate for you again. Still… it can be a bit boring wandering around alone.*

"Sure. Do you have a map of Capri?"

"Yeah, I picked one up from the hotel in Amalfi. I asked Marco what some must see sights are and marked them on the map."

"Sounds good. Lead the way." I stepped to the side to let her pass.

Everywhere we went had a breathtaking view of the spectacularly blue sea. The houses and gardens were immaculately presented, the streets (although sometimes narrow and steep) were spotlessly clean and the air was incredibly fresh. We stopped often to take pictures and to sit on a bench just to enjoy the view of the sea and listen to the waves below.

I was leaning on the rail, trying to take a picture of the waves hitting the cliffside, when someone called out Jessica's name. A woman in her forties, and a slightly shorter version of herself that could only be her daughter, were chatting with Jessica. I knew them by sight and from their accent guessed they were Australian, but we hadn't spoken before.

"Hey, this is Erica and her mum Anne. They're from Sydney too."

"Hi, nice to meet you."

Two black, shoulder length bobs nodded.

"We're looking for the pizzeria Marco recommended. Would you like to join us?" said Anne.

"We were looking for that too." Jessica looked at me. "We could split the bill between the four of us."

I smiled and nodded. Finding the place took a little longer than expected, and by the time I placed our order in Italian, we were all famished but had only ordered one margarita pizza for €15. Pretending I was full from the two very thin slices, I settled the bill and we went for a walk before heading back to the meeting spot.

As soon as the ferry began moving, I wished I hadn't eaten any lunch. The sea sickness was worse than the trip to Capri, and the worst part was I had to endure it for longer – all the way to Rome.

Clutching my stomach, I took shallow breaths and cursed sea travel.

If I had known I got sea sick, I would have bought tablets!

Everyone else laughed and chatted about their day, while I sweated and tried not to vomit. I was the first passenger to disembark. Thankfully, the bus ride to the hotel was short and I had recovered enough to spend some time in the lobby saying goodbye to Maria and her family. I was about to step into the elevator when Marco called me over.

"Noor, you are staying in Rome tomorrow, yes?"

"Yes, but just for one day."

Marco nodded. "There are few others staying in this hotel and want to go around Rome tomorrow. I can introduce you, and maybe if you like you can go together?"

"Yeah, that would be great. Thanks!"

I didn't mind exploring Rome on my own, but it was a large city and a little intimidating. This way I could enjoy the company of some familiar faces.

"This is George and Helen from South Africa, and Tim and Mary from New Zealand –"

"We've met and chatted before," Mary said with a smile.

"Excellent! And this is Rose from Adelaide. Noor is fluent in Italian. Maybe if you buy her lunch she will be your tour guide tomorrow." Marco chuckled at his own joke. "I must go help the others. Very nice to meet you all, and Noor if you want to become tour guide, let me know."

"Thanks Marco, it was nice to meet you!"

I arranged to meet the others in the lobby tomorrow morning and went up to my room.

I'll just lie down for a minute, so my stomach can stop spinning.

The next thing I knew, it was almost eight and dark outside. I gnawed my lip. The hotel was outside the centre of Rome, and walking in the dark did not seem like a good idea.

Annoyed at myself for falling asleep, I walked down to the restaurant.

It was mostly empty, and when I looked at the menu I could guess why.

"Um, excuse me?" I called out in Italian. "I know it's not on the menu, but could I have a salad? I'll pay for it, of course."

His thick, dark eyebrows pulled together. "A what?"

I cleared my throat. "A salad. Just some lettuce leaves and a tomato. Sorry for the trouble, it's just – I wasn't feeling well … "

And the only thing I can afford on your menu is a salad. I hope…

The waiter sighed, snatched the menu from my hand and went into the kitchen.

"Hello Noor."

I turned in my chair. "Oh, hello … "

Oh no! I can't remember their names!

"Have you finished eating?" The Malaysian father asked.

His wife and three sons stood behind him smiling shyly.

"No, I've just ordered."

"Join us," he invited. "We can all eat together."

The waiter had reappeared, a surly frown on his face.

"Chef says you can have salad. It will take 15 minutes."

"Thank you."

The Malaysian father waved at a larger table then pointed at me. "We all sit here together?"

"Come dice?" the waiter asked. *(What are you saying?)*

"He would like us all to sit together," I translated.

"But I have to move your things, add another plate and cutlery!"

"Come, come," The Malaysian father said, pulling out my chair. "Join us."

I just wanted a quick dinner before going back to my room …

The started re-setting the table with an extra plate, muttering under his breath.

"So, this is last night in Rome. You enjoy the trip?"

"Yes. Um, I'm so sorry – This is so embarrassing. I forgot your names …"

They laughed. "Is okay. There are five of us and we only have to remember one name. I am Firash, this is wife Delima and my sons Aqil, Umar and Ayiz."

"Yes, of course. I'm so sorry!"

We chatted about the trip and Delima told me about all the beautiful things she had bought. Firash complained about how much she had spent on leather handbags and gold. The boys talked amongst themselves quietly.

The waiter appeared with a large glass mixing bowl full of wilted salad leaves and shrivelled slices of tomatoes. Firash tried to order roast chicken and chips, but after several attempts I stepped in and translated that they could not eat meat because it wasn't Halal and could the chef please roast a chicken large enough for five people?

The waiter threw up his hands and stormed off to the kitchen. I smiled apologetically at the family and directed their thoughts back to the trip until the dry chicken and chips appeared almost an hour later.

"So your parents let you travel alone? They not scared?" Delima asked.

"They do worry, but we have family here and I'm on an organized tour. It's pretty safe."

"Very nice parents," Firash said, wiping his mouth and thick moustache on the cloth napkin. "They give you trip as gift for getting into university?"

I laughed. "No, we're too poor for extravagant gifts like that. I have been working and saving money since I was fourteen just for this trip. I wanted to see my family and friends again."

"What?" Delima gasped. "They let children work in Australia?"

Firash looked at his oldest son. "That is your age. Why you no work like her and instead spend all my money?"

Delima smacked his arm and said something in Malay.

"What work did you do?" Aqil asked, peering over his glasses.

"The usual stuff. Babysitting, waitressing and working in shops as a sales assistant. It took a *long* time to save up."

Firash and Delima nodded their heads.

"Wow, is amazing. You are young but know how hard money is to earn." Firash bobbed his head. "And all to see your family."

"You are good girl," Delima said.

I smiled and asked them about what life was like in Malaysia. It seemed as unusual and fascinating to me that teenagers didn't generally have part time jobs, as my working did to them. When they finished eating, Firash insisted on paying for my salad to thank me for translating and they wished me well on the rest of my trip, inviting me to visit them if I was ever in Malaysia.

Smiling, I thanked them for the food and their enjoyable company. Instead of eating alone in an overpriced restaurant, my last night on tour had turned out to be more enjoyable than expected. I waved goodbye until the elevator doors closed and went back to my room to sleep. Mary, Tim and the others wanted to start early tomorrow so we could take our time enjoying Rome.

CHAPTER 7
ALL ROADS LEAD BACK TO ROME

Rose was already in the lobby when I arrived.

"Good morning," she said with a smile and a wave.

I waved back. "Morning. We must be early."

She nodded towards the elevator behind me. "George and Helen are just arriving."

"Good morning," said George then nodded at me. "Thank you for agreeing to translate for us today. It makes things so much easier than trying to use a phrasebook."

I smiled. "No worries. It's nice to have some company to explore a big city like Rome, but I have to warn you that I'm terrible at reading maps."

Helen laughed. "That's okay. You just translate for us and George can do the navigating. He's very good at reading maps."

"Mary's coming," Ruth announced with a nod towards the elevators.

"Where's Tim?" George asked when Mary reached our little group.

"Sleeping in," Mary said with a laugh. "He wants to rest before our flight tonight."

"Ours leaves in the afternoon so we need to come back here around twelve," George said.

I nodded and adjusted my backpack. "That doesn't leave us much time to explore. Is there anything in particular anyone wants to see?"

"Trevi Fountain" George said immediately.

Helen nodded. "We hardly got to see it during that dinner."

"I would love to see the Spanish Steps," Rose added.

"Was it just me or did it feel like our day in Rome was a bit rushed? Mary asked.

"It was. And the dinner that first night was overpriced," George said.

"Well, how would you like to get there?" I pulled out my pocket map of Rome. "I think the hotel is just outside the city. We could catch a taxi or try public transport?"

"I'm happy to try the public transport," Mary said. "The taxis here are so expensive."

"I'm fine with public transport too," Rose said.

I looked at George and Helen who nodded.

"All right, I'll go ask the reception desk how to get there."

I left the others chatting and walked over to the reception desk. The concierge explained we would have to catch a bus that would take us to the metro station, which would then take us into the city. It seemed a bit complicated but he assured me it was easy and marked them on the map.

Surprisingly everything went more smoothly than I had anticipated, from buying the tickets to navigating the public transport system.

We strolled through the paved streets of Rome, stopping frequently to take pictures of each other and the landmarks. Much to my companion's delight, I found a bar (Italian café`) that only charged €1 for a cappuccino and after a brief rest, we headed to the Trevi fountain.

It was spectacular. The statues were so detailed I half expected them to move.

"Why is it empty?" George asked.

I glanced down and my mouth dropped open. "Where's all the water gone?"

"The fountain was what we wanted to see most and we have to go soon …"

"I think they were cleaning it," Rose said. "We could wait and see if they re-fill it."

"There's the cleaning crew," Mary tapped my shoulder.

I looked in the direction she was pointing and walked over to them. A quick chat gave me all the information I needed.

"Well, the good news is they will start refilling it now but the bad news is it takes at least half an hour," I told the group.

George and Helen looked at each other, then at their watches.

"We could stay, but we would have to catch a taxi back to the hotel," George told Helen.

She nodded. "It will be worth it."

We watched the water slowly fill the fountain, and every now and then George would glance at his watch but they stayed until it was almost half full. By now, other tourists were gathering and pulling out coins from their bags.

"Does everyone have a coin?" Mary asked.

I grinned and nodded. "I hope the legend is right. I'd love to come back one day."

George and Helen stayed long enough to toss their coins into the water, wished us a safe trip home and rushed off to find a taxi.

"Is there anything else you would like to see?" I asked Mary and Rose.

"I'd love to see Piazza Navona," Rose said.

"I'm happy to walk around and just look at the build-ings," Mary said. "But can we get some lunch first?"

"Do you think you can find us another bargain like that cappuccino?" Rose asked. "I don't mind street food."

"Me either," Mary said.

I laughed. "I'll try. Why don't we start walking to the Piazza and I'll keep a lookout for anything along the way?"

They nodded and Rose, having taken over George's role, took the lead with the map.

We walked and walked until our feet ached, but we saw everything that was on our wish list. We even got a short history lesson from one of the Carabinieri (policeman), on guard duty in Piazza Navona. By the time I found an affordable meal, my stomach was growling. The food truck had three bustling women behind the counter, a long line of customers and several choices of sandwiches, pizza and schnitzels with steamed vegetables. We crowded around one of the small, round tables in front of the truck and ate standing up.

"Not bad. Better than a lot of places we stopped to eat at, and way cheaper!" Mary said and wiped her mouth on a napkin.

Rose was looking at the sky. "It's starting to get dark. Maybe we should head back to the hotel? Unless there is somewhere else we should visit?"

"I've seen everything I wanted to," Mary told her. "Besides, Tim will be wondering if I got lost in Rome."

I nodded. "I'll just grab some pizza for my dinner and we'll head off."

WE NAVIGATED the metro easily enough, but by the time we were on the bus heading back to the hotel it was dark enough that I struggled to read the signs outside.

"Is the next stop ours?" Rose asked.

I squinted, my nose flat against the window. "Yes, I think so. Better ring the bell."

Mary pulled the cord but the bus didn't slow down and drove right past our stop.

"Oh, maybe the driver thought we meant the next stop …" Mary sounded a little nervous.

"Don't worry," I told them. "We'll get off at the next stop and walk back. It can't be far."

The bus kept driving.

We pressed our faces against the windows trying to spot the next bus stop, but there was an only open field.

"Is that sheep?" Mary asked. "Yes, I'm sure it's sheep."

My stomach flipped. "Ummm … I'll ask someone."

I turned to the woman sitting next to us. "Scusi, we were supposed to get off at the last stop. Where is the next stop?"

"Ah, you were supposed to get off at the last stop of the city! You missed it."

I gulped. "Where are we? Where is the bus going?"

"You're in countryside around Rome."

"Oh no!" I whispered.

How am I going to tell Rose and Mary I got us lost in the countryside at night?

"Don't worry," the woman reassured me. "The next stop is coming soon. Get off there, cross the road and wait at bus stop on other site. That will take you back to city."

Relief swept through my body. Mary and Rose were watching me with worried looks so I flashed them a smile and a thumb up.

"How often do the buses for Rome go by?"

She shrugged. "Maybe 15 minutes, maybe 30."

"Thank you so much!"

"Prego. Buona Fortuna." *(You're welcome. Good luck.)*

I EXPLAINED the situation to Rose and Mary, apologizing several times, and we got off at the next stop as the woman had instructed.

"Wow, we really are in the Roman countryside," Rose commented, looking around. "We haven't seen anyone go past the whole time we've been here."

I glanced at my watch. We'd been waiting, huddled

together against the cold in the bus shelter, for over fifteen minutes. "I'm so sorry about this …"

Mary waved a hand. "Relax, we all missed the stop. It was hard to see."

"No harm done and we even get to experience the roman country side," Rose said.

A sheep bleated in agreement.

"You've shown us more of Rome than the actual tour we did," Mary said.

"We even got to see Roman sheep," Rose added.

They laughed but I couldn't join in.

What if the bus doesn't come? What if it comes too late and they miss their flight? It will be my fault!

"Maybe we should call for a taxi," I suggested. "I don't want you to miss your flight."

"Let's wait five more minutes and then we'll call the taxi," Rose said.

"There it is! It's coming!" Mary pointed to the horizon.

We cheered and stepped out onto the road, waving our arms to get the driver's attention. There was no way this bus was going to go past us.

I stood next to the bus driver the whole way so I could be sure we got off at the right stop. He was kind enough to drop us off very close to our hotel and after a short walk, we said our goodbyes and well wishes in the lobby and parted ways.

I WENT UP to my room, tired and hungry, but my cold pizza didn't seem to be as appetising as when I bought it. There was no microwave in my room and after a few bites; I spent the next twenty minutes trying to warm up the pizza with my hairdryer before giving up and eating it cold.

I spent the evening packing my suitcase while chatting to my family on the phone, then called grandma.

"Pronto?" *(Hello?)*

"Nonna, it's me." *(Grandma)*

"Ciao gioia! Where are you now?" *(Hello dear.)*

"My hotel in Rome. The tour finished and I'm coming to Pollone tomorrow."

"I know, I wrote the date down and put it on the fridge."

I laughed. "Are you coming to get me?"

"No, I'm making lunch – stuffed zucchini flowers. Your Uncle Francesco will pick you up from the airport."

"Okay. I should be at your house by lunchtime!"

"You better get some sleep. You have an early flight tomorrow."

"Wait! What if Uncle Francesco doesn't recognise me?"

"What? How could he not recognise you?"

"It's been almost nine years since we left. I was little then."

"We know what you look like! Your parents sent us pictures of you and your sister."

"What if *I* don't recognise *him*? I don't have a recent picture of him!"

"Stop worrying! If you don't recognise your uncle, he'll know you. Now go to sleep."

I rolled my eyes. "Fine, fine. Goodnight grandma, see you tomorrow."

"Sogni d'oro." *(Golden dreams/sweet dreams.)*

CHAPTER 8
A SMALL VILLAGE IN THE ALPS

G randma was right. Uncle Francesco recognised me immediately.

" Ciao Noor!" He called out, waving his arm high in the air. "Over here!"

I grinned and waved back. Even if he hadn't recognised me, I would have recognised him. He hadn't changed much, except for a bit more grey in his hair.

"Welcome back!" He said, patting my shoulder. "I can't believe how much you've grown. You were this high - " he held his palm waist high above the ground " - when you left Italy."

"Marina is even taller than me," I told him. "But only a little bit."

It had always annoyed me that my younger sister was taller.

"Really? My kids are taller than you too. Looks like you're the shortest one in the family."

"Hmpf. Yeah, well, Napoleon and Alexander the Great were short too. And anyway, Federica and Manuele are both older than me so of course they're taller. But I could still grow!"

He laughed and reached for the suitcase handle. "Let's go, your grandma has been waiting since the crack of dawn."

"How are Frederica and Manuele?"

"Good, good. They each have their own apartments now and full time jobs. I'll take you to see them on the weekend."

He led the way to the car park, pulling my suitcase behind him.

"Are we riding on your motorcycle?"

He chuckled. "No, no. Too cold and no room for a suitcase. I brought my Fiat."

As soon as we were in the car with seatbelts on, Uncle Francesco lit a cigarette and lowered the window next to him. A blast of icy air entered the car, but it was better than inhaling the cigarette smoke.

"Does Grandma know you still smoke?"

"Yeah. She hates it. Keeps telling me to stop but I'm too old to quit."

He inhaled on the cigarette and blew the smoke out of the slightly opened window.

I wrinkled my nose. His efforts to direct the smoke out of the car was appreciated, but not very effective.

"How long until we reach Pollone?"

"One hour if the traffic isn't bad."

I spent the next hour breathing through my thick scarf, pulling it down slightly to ask questions or answer his.

"We're driving through Biella, aren't we?"

Uncle Francesco glanced at me, eyebrows raised in surprise. "Ha! You remember quite a lot, don't you?"

"We used to buy the best pizza slices somewhere around here, and come to the market on Saturdays."

"Do you remember where cousin Angela's house is?"

"Not really, but I remember the house and the garden very clearly." I grinned. "I remember running around the garden with her kids and trying to pat their cats. I think they had six or seven cats."

"Vittoria and Pietro are both at university now. I know they are a few years older than you, but I forget exactly how old they are. I'll take you to see them when you've settled in. Angela has already called your grandma and invited you over for lunch."

I nodded and smiled. I had loved playing with Vittoria and Pietro, scrambling up the steep gardens full of fruit trees and watching Disney movies together, then having some of Angela's home-made fruit jam brioche. I couldn't wait to see them again.

The Fiat made its way up the gradually increasing mountain slope towards Pollone and soon we were driving through the paved and narrow village streets.

"I know where we are!" I shifted forward in my seat and pointed out of the windscreen. "Around the corner is the library."

Uncle Francesco nodded. "Very good. Do you think you could find your way to grandma's house from here?"

"Yes, I'm sure I can. That's the post office," I pointed to the wooden door on the street corner. "And the butcher's shop and… that's my old primary school!"

Uncle Francesco nodded approvingly and smiled. "It's impressive you remember so much."

I leaned back in my chair and grinned. I could hear the water of the river flowing through the slightly open window. The air was crisp and clean, perfumed with the scent of pine trees.

"What's this river called?"

"Oremo."

"There's another one closer to grandma's house, isn't there?"

"Yes, Vandorba, but that's a little brook."

"I remember that little shop," I pointed out the side of the window. "Does grandma still by her bread from there?"

"Every morning."

The Fiat worked hard to get up the steep driveway that led to Grandma's house. I leaned forward, my breath catching. Everything was exactly as I remembered it. To the left, the woodshed was piled high with enough logs to last three winters. I could hear the cows in their stall next to the woodshed, their enormous pile of hay filling the adjacent barn. All the farm houses were attached to these buildings, still empty and slightly more dilapidated. At the end of the courtyard was the enormous metal gate, its bright red colour faded to copper. My grandmother's house was at the end of the courtyard, right next to the red gate. She has been renting it for as long as I can remember and nothing had changed over the years. The same rickety wooden ladder leaned against the hayloft where she kept her logs for the winter. On the ground level was the outdoor toilet/shower cubicle with the metal door and frosted glass window.

I had never seen a similar bathroom arrangement anywhere else. The toilet was at the back of the small cubicle, and to use it I had to walk through the shower area, which was impossible to use in winter because the water froze in the pipes. It was a wonder the toilet plumbing still worked in winter. Just in front of the toilet was the creaky, rusty outdoor metal staircase that led up to the two bedrooms. Directly underneath them were the two rooms of the house; the kitchen/meal/living area and the room next to it that Grandma always kept closed off and in immaculate condition. The outdoor stone sink with makeshift roof cover was still there, its pipes wrapped in thick cloth in a futile attempt to stop the water freezing. I smiled. How many times had I helped grandma wash our clothes there? I would stand on the tip of my toes and hand her the soap while she scrubbed them against the stone surface.

The car had barely stopped in the gravelled courtyard when the door flew open and Grandma rushed out in her slippers, closely followed by Gigi. I fumbled with my seat belt and stumbled out of the car, blinking rapidly to stop tears from escaping.

"You're here! You're here!" She clapped her hands together. "Finally!"

I stared at her in shock. When I left she had towered over me, tall and proud looking with sharp blue eyes and carefully arranged, dyed blond hair.

"Nonna …" I breathed and enveloped her thin frame in a hug, careful not to squeeze too hard and break her. "You've shrunk! And your hair is all white."

Smack!

"Ouch!" I rubbed the back of my head and grinned. Some things don't change and it was good to know that Grandma wasn't as fragile as she looked.

"It's my turn to hug her Anna," Gigi said, wiping away his tears.

"Gigi!" I grinned. "What a nice surprise! I didn't know you were going to be here."

His enthusiastic hug almost crushed my ribs.

"Of course I was going to be here to welcome you back. You've been gone so long! And your dad is my best friend, he's like a brother to me." He blew his nose in a handkerchief.

I bit the inside of my cheek. Seeing people cry always makes me want to cry too. Desperate to lighten the mood, I tried to think of something funny to say but Gigi was still talking.

"You told us that you would come back, even though you were so little. You said you would and now here you are," he spoke through his tears.

"Of course I came back! I promised I would."

"Yes, but you were so young when you left that you could have forgotten all about us," Grandma pointed out a little sadly.

"Listen to her Italian!" Gigi said happily, "She hasn't forgotten anything, she speaks better than we do. What about Piemontese? Can you speak that too?"

I shook my head. "Dad only taught us Italian, but I can understand a little bit."

Gigi blew his nose loudly in his checked handkerchief.

"My lunch break is almost over, but I'll come back to see you soon," Gigi promised.

"Thank you for coming to see me. Say hi to Luisa and the cats for me."

He nodded, crushed my ribs one last time and walked to his car wiping away tears.

I WAVED goodbye until he had left the courtyard then followed Grandma and Uncle Francesco into the house. Even here nothing had changed. The same rectangular table took up most of the small, square room with the same hard couch against the left wall. On the opposite wall, the wood fire stove crackled cheerfully. Next to it, the stone sink was hidden from view by the cupboard doors. There was just enough room next to the front door for the fridge and television.

It was like stepping back into my childhood.

Grandma opened the doors to the adjacent room and tilted her head towards it.

"We put a bed in there for you. And installed a wood pellet heater because your uncle said you wouldn't be used to sleeping in a cold room. I told him that you used to sleep upstairs with me all the time when you were little."

"She's not used to the cold after living in Australia for so long," Uncle Francesco said in his mild manner. "Besides, she's 18 now and doesn't want to go to sleep at 7 PM like you do. At least down here she can stay up and watch TV."

"Bah! TV! Sleeping early is good for your health," Grandma grumbled and walked into the formal dining room.

I followed her, pausing at the threshold. My Grandpa had made all the furniture in this room before he died, and all these years Grandma had kept it spotless and neat. We had never been allowed to play in here, or even used it as a dining room, but now it was going to be my bedroom.

A single bed was pushed against the left wall. Next to it

was the door that led to the courtyard and the outdoor toilet, hidden by a lacy curtain.

"I had this installed just for you," Grandma told me, pointing to a big, metal contraption.

I watched a few pellets fall into the burner and be consumed by the bright yellow and red flames. The room was deliciously warm.

I leaned over and kissed her wrinkled cheek.

Uncle Francesco walked to the other side of the small room and picked up a stack of CDs. "Do you like Enya? There's some Italian pop songs too."

"Your uncle bought you that CD player because he thought you would be bored here," Grandma commented before I could answer him.

"I know you like reading, and I have a lot of books you can borrow to pass the time. And you can use the shower in my apartment when you want to. I've given your grandma a copy of my house keys. It's not far, you can walk there and make yourself at home."

Grandma made a tutting noise. "I've always washed in a tub in front of the stove and managed just fine."

I remembered that large wash tub from my childhood. First, we had to build a fire and then heat the water in a large pot. Mum or Grandma would help us wash by pouring buckets of warm water over our heads.

"She is used to a shower," Uncle Francesco argued back, then rolled his eyes at me. "Your Grandma still lives in ancient times."

"Hmpf," she muttered his way before pointing under my bed. "I put a chamber pot under there for you."

I remembered the chamber pot too and cringed. Upstairs in the two bedrooms (where there is no heating), we had to use chamber pots during the night because the stairs would be too slippery with snow or ice to risk walking down to the outdoor toilet.

"Why can't I just use the toilet? It's right outside this door."

"Because it's cold outside," Grandma told me sharply. "What if you slipped on ice or snow? Besides, you would have to unlock the door of this room, and unlock the toilet, and then remember to lock them both when you come back in. You would need a flashlight and you would freeze to death before you made it there and back."

"I'm not using the chamber pot," I told her stubbornly.

I had hated using it as a child, and I was prepared to risk a bladder infection rather than use it again.

Uncle Francesco shook his head and chortled. "Give her a copy of the door keys. I'll bring over a flashlight tonight."

Grandma threw her hands up in the air. "Fine! Come and eat lunch."

It was good to be back.

GRANDMA SPENT the afternoon on the phone, calling her sister-in-law, niece and nephew in Veneto to announce my arrival and putting me on the receiver to chat with them. I remembered them from holidays in my early childhood, but wouldn't see them on this trip. Travelling in winter was difficult for Grandma so we made do with phone calls. Angela, Enzo and Amalia called to organize a short visit in the next couple of days. Grandma pursed her lips but she could hardly say no to her nephew and his wife, or her cousin Angela.

"I'll hardly get to see you," she muttered, folding the cloth napkins after dinner. "Everyone is inviting you over for lunches and dinners. And when do I get to spend time with you?"

"I'm here for three months nonna. You're going to be sick of me by then."

"Go brush your teeth. We'll watch the evening news and then go to bed."

I would have argued that 8 o'clock was too early for sleep

but I was already yawning. Who knew that coach tours could be so exhausting?

THE CHURCH BELLS ringing woke me up every hour that night, but I didn't mind. It was comforting to hear familiar sounds and I knew that soon I wouldn't notice them anymore. I didn't even mind fumbling with the keys and flashlight to use the outdoor toilet. The cold was manageable if I remembered to wear a couple of wool jumpers before opening the door. And it was all infinitely better than using the chamber pot under my bed.

The rooster's crowing woke me up and I lay shivering under the blankets. My heater was turned off and I didn't know how to start it, but I knew how to light a fire in the wood stove. I was pretty sure I did. I mean, I had watched Grandma light the stove hundreds of times when I was a child. How hard could it be?

I strained my ears but heard no movement upstairs.

She must still be sleeping. Wouldn't it be a nice surprise for her to come down to a warm kitchen?

Pulling on a thick wool jumper, I moved quietly towards the stove.

Wood neatly stacked in a basket by the stove - check.

Matches – check.

Old newspaper – check.

Humming a little tune, I shredded the newspaper and put it in the belly of the stove. The trick to lighting a fire is to light the newspaper before adding the wood. At least that's how I remembered it. I lit bunch after bunch of shredded newspaper, yelping occasionally when the flames on the matchsticks touched my fingertips, but the wooden log refused to catch fire.

THUMP!

I jumped, accidentally dropping the lit match onto the tiles and looked up. The thumping was moving across the ceiling, then thundering down the stairs.

The door flew open.

Grandma stood in her nightgown with only a shawl around her shoulders and a horrified look on her face.

"What are you doing?" She shrieked, pointing at me.

I looked down. I was surrounded by used matches and shredded paper, and there was a little smoke coming out of the stove.

"It was supposed to be a surprise for when you woke up... "

Grandma clutched her heart. "Don't ever do that again!" She ordered sternly. "You'll burn yourself and burn the house down."

"I know how to light a fire!" I said very indignantly.

Walking to the cupboard behind me, she pulled out a box of what looked like giant sugar cubes that smelled strongly of gasoline.

"You have to put this in first, light it under the newspaper, and *then* you add small pieces of wood to get the fire going. Not that giant log you were trying to burn!"

"Ah, yes, well … Ahem. It must be a new way of doing it, but now that I know I can get the fire going for you every morning," I offered enthusiastically.

Her pale skin turned white. "No, no," she said hurriedly. "You sleep in and enjoy your university holidays. I wake up at dawn anyway, so I will come down and light the fire before you are even awake."

"But I want to help –"

"No need, I've managed all these years on my own. You don't touch the fire!"

"Okay, well I will chop the wood for you."

"No!!" She yelled in alarm. "You will cut off your leg with the axe!"

"I've chopped wood for you before," I reminded her,

rolling my eyes. "When I was younger too. I am sure I can do it even better now."

"Don't touch the axe!" She snapped. "I remember how clumsy you are. And I intend on sending you back to your parents in one piece, just as you came. Besides, I can do it all myself."

"What about the big logs? They are too big for you to chop. I can do that."

"Your uncle chops the big pieces for me."

"But I can help! And I've chopped wood before, it's not that hard –"

"Absolutely not. It's too dangerous. You haven't lived here for years. You don't know how to do these things properly and we don't want any accidents."

There was no point arguing. Apparently living in Australia had made me soft and unused to mountain living. Even if there was some truth to it, I refused to admit it.

"Since you're up, get dressed and we will go down to Roberta's shop to buy fresh bread - remind me to get biscuits for visitors - Remember Roberta? She's looking forward to seeing you, and while we are there you can say hello to everyone else too."

"Everyone else? I just got here! How would they know I'm here?"

"I've been telling everyone that you're coming," Grandma said as though it was obvious.

"When do we go see grandpa?"

"After lunch. And we'll stop to buy some flowers along the way."

I smiled. The monthly cemetery visits I remembered always included flowers. Grandma would chat to Grandpa, point out how quickly my sister and I were growing and clean his tomb. Most of our ancestors were also buried there, in a family tomb with the majestic snow-capped mountains as a backdrop.

What a shame he died before I was born, I thought a little sadly. *But if he's watching, he'll know we care about him.*

ENZO AND AMALIA arrived on the dot of the appointed hour.

"Ciao zia," Enzo kissed grandma on the cheek and gave me a big hug. *(Hello aunty.)*

"Look how much you've grown! You were this high when you left – Ah, if only my mum could see you now!" he said.

I swallowed the lump that had manifested in my throat. "I'd like to go visit great aunt Denise's grave, and take her some flowers."

He nodded, wiping the tears leaking from his eyes on a large handkerchief. "She would like that. She loved you and your sister so much."

I patted him on the shoulder while he blew his nose loudly. "We still have all the kinder surprise toys from the chocolate eggs she gave us every Sunday."

"Do you really?"

"Yes, and we both remember how she would stand looking out her window, waiting for us every Sunday afternoon. We were so upset we couldn't come to the funeral."

Amalia walked in, wearing one of her fur coats and battle face. She exchanged slightly frosty greetings with Grandma, who was pressing her lips tightly together, and smothered me with hugs and kisses.

Not having children of their own, Enzo and Amalia had always lavished my younger sister and I with love and attention. We had loved visiting their house and playing with them. Enzo would roast chestnuts on an open fire in the garden and feed us honey from his beehives. Amalia would tell us stories, make us hot chocolate and give us lots of cuddles. I missed them a lot and for years, I wrote them letters about my new life in Australia, promising to return one day.

Amalia eventually released me and sat down, elegantly

dabbing away tears. She neatly folded her white handkerchief with embroidered flowers and eyed Grandma with a steely gaze.

"Anna, you can't have Noor all the time. I want her to spend two weeks with me."

"Two weeks!" Grandma exploded.

Cringing, I retreated to the back wall next to Enzo who was looking slightly anxious.

Amalia had come prepared for battle. "You can't have her for the whole 3 months!"

"I'm not! She's already going away for *a whole week* to stay with her friends in Brescia, and now you expect me to let her go for another two weeks? Then I will only have 2 months!"

"You have to share."

"No I don't," Grandma snapped. "I'm her grandmother and she came all this way to see *me*."

The dresser pressed against my back. I held my breath, trying not to draw attention to myself. Enzo wiped his forehead and stayed silent. He knew better than to get in between an argument with his aunt and wife. Unfortunately for us, there was nowhere to hide.

Amalia, sitting at the dining table, did not even flinch from Grandma's fierce glare. How can someone so old and tiny look so fearsome?

They narrowed their eyes at each other.

"12 days," Amalia compromised through gritted teeth.

"3 days," Grandma's voice was like a whip.

Amalia laughed incredulously, completely unfazed, and counter offered, "10 days."

Enzo and I glanced at each other and let out a low nervous laugh. If I had money to bet, I would have bet on Grandma getting her way. My parents tell me I'm stubborn, but I obviously got it from somewhere and the apple doesn't fall far from the tree.

"10 days?! 10 days? No! Utterly ridiculous. When am I

supposed to see her? I'm old and will die soon. You can see her anytime."

"Don't be ridiculous, *you* will live forever! You have plenty of time to see her, 10 days is hardly any time at all. I already prepared her room."

"No, no it's impossible."

"You can't keep her with you all the time like a prisoner!"

Enzo and I winced. The room seemed to shrink and get hotter as Grandma and Amalia shot daggers at each other with their eyes.

"5 days," Grandma snapped. "That's almost a whole week."

Perhaps sensing she would not get a better offer, Amalia snatched the opportunity. "Done! 5 days with me, but I also get to have her over for some day visits."

"Not during Christmas or her birthday."

They stared at each other for a few seconds before Amalia said, "You're a hard woman to bargain with Anna."

Grandma took that as a compliment. Having won her battle, she remembered to show some hospitality to her nephew and his wife.

"Coffee?" she offered a little too smugly.

Amalia pursed her lips but accepted the coffee with good grace.

Personally, I was surprised Grandma had agreed to five days, and without any bloodshed. Enzo looked as relieved as I felt, and thankfully the rest of the visit passed smoothly.

THE NEXT FEW days brought a steady stream of visitors. Dad's childhood friends came to welcome me back and brought gifts for me and to take home to my parents and sister. My favourite was a wedding video of one of dad's friends who had been single for many years. They made me promise to tell them how long it would take him to work out that it was a prank. I was very impressed with the trouble they took to stage an elaborate faux wedding, complete with veil and bridegroom.

I could see why they were friends with my dad. Just like him, they hadn't lost their sense of humour or fun. Best of all was the information they gave me on dad, specifically all the naughty things he did when he was my age.

Just wait until I get back home and he tells me I can't do something because I'm too young or I don't have enough experience or it's too dangerous.

Grandma behaved as a gracious hostess during the visits, making coffee and offering biscuits with the occasional smile, but she was happiest when it was just the two of us.

CHAPTER 9
PEACE AND TRANQUILLITY,
MOST OF THE TIME...

We quickly settled into a daily routine. More accurately, Grandma settled me into *her* daily routine which seemed to follow the hours of a nursing home. While the church bells were still announcing the seventh hour, she would already be lighting the wood stove. After a light breakfast of warm milk with honey and children's vitamin infused biscuits (which we both loved), we would walk down the drive and cross the narrow street to Roberta's bakery / mini supermarket for freshly baked bread. Depending on what day it was, she would either do laundry, clean and tidy or teach me how to cook. If I didn't have a cooking lesson scheduled, I would read or listen to music in my room while she watched the mid-morning news, or clamber over the hill backing onto Grandma's house and sit by the pond in the nature reserve, Parco Burcina. Once a week, Uncle Francesco would give us a lift to the butcher's shop before going to work. The rest of the afternoon would pass by quietly as Grandma and I would talk, read books, watch TV and entertain the occasional visitor. Dinner was at six o'clock, followed by the evening news and then she would go to bed by eight thirty while I stayed up to read and watch television.

. . .

It had been a long time since Grandma had lived with an eighteen year old and she wasn't quite sure what to do with me. I would spend most of the day sprawled on the hard vinyl couch, steadily making my way through the pile of novels uncle Francesco had lent me.

"You shouldn't read so much," she muttered, rearranging her things next to the faded pink rotary telephone. "You'll make yourself go blind."

"That's not true," I argued. "Besides, what else am I supposed to do? You won't let me help you with laundry, or chop the wood and we're not having a cooking lesson today."

"You're supposed to be on holidays, not working like a maid."

"But this is what I do on holidays." I said, waving the book. "Anyway, it's good for me to practice reading in Italian."

"The only book I read is by Saint Pio," Grandma said, pointing to the thick book by the phone. "It's a wonderful book. You should read it some time."

I eyed it dubiously. Somehow, I didn't think that the preachings of a saint would hold much interest for me.

"Thanks… but I already have so many books to get through."

"I'm going to have a bath today. You should wash too."

"I'm not washing in that old tin tub."

"Why not? You used to when you were little."

"I'll wait for the weekend and use Uncle Francesco's shower."

She sighed and glanced at the wall clock. "Go for a walk," she suggested.

I smirked. "Time for the news?"

"Walking is healthy for you. You're young, you should be more active!"

"Ha! You just want me out of the house so you can watch the news in peace. Why didn't you just tell me to turn the music down?"

"I don't know how you can listen to music so loud. You'll make yourself deaf."

"Why do you bother with the news? It will be the same as this morning's news *and* it will be the same this afternoon and evening."

"Nonsense! Something might happen. How else are we supposed to know what's going on?"

I rolled my eyes. "I'll go up to Burcina."

She nodded approvingly. "Wear your coat and scarf, it's cold outside. And stay a bit longer. I might as well have my bath while you're out."

"Enjoy the peace and quiet while I'm gone," I chuckled.

"Lunch is at twelve, don't be late!"

"I know, I know! It's *always* at twelve… " I muttered under my breath.

The climb up the hill was steep, but it was a great shortcut and in a few minutes I was sitting by the pond watching the turtles and fish swim around. My shoulders loosened and I leaned back into the bench. As much as I loved Grandma, her insistence on watching every news update during the day drove me crazy. Although, to be fair, I probably drove her crazy when I played loud music in my room. Poor Grandma. All she wanted was to listen to the news, while I tried my best *not* to listen to the repetitive depressing stories. Going out for a walk during news time was a much better alternative for both of us.

MY FAVOURITE DAY of the week was Wednesday, when the new issue of Topolino came out. The popular cartoon comic book, full of the adventures of Mickey Mouse and his friends, also came in a version for girls with Minnie as the protagonist. Unfortunately for me, they were not available in Australia so I was making up for lost time.

"Nonna, I'm going to the newsagent," I said, heading to the door.

"Wrap your scarf properly or you will get a cold," she responded without looking up from her ironing.

She still used irons made of cast iron. They came in several sizes and had to be warmed up on the wood fire stove, then placed on a plain cotton cloth that acted as a barrier between the iron and our clothes. They were heavy and it took a long time to heat them but Grandma insisted they did a better job than the modern electric ones. I loved watching her iron but I was in a rush today- I didn't want to miss out on a copy of the Topolino Christmas special.

I opened the front door and gasped.

A massive pink pig stared at me, his nose inching closer to my jacket. I stumbled back in surprise and he took it as an invitation to enter, using his unfair advantage of surprise and bulk to push me back and step over the threshold.

"Close the door, you're letting all the cold air in!" Grandma scolded.

"I can't!" I shifted my body slightly, trying to block Piggy's progress into the room.

Tutting impatiently, she placed the iron on the wood fire stove and moved toward me.

"What are you doing? Close the door before we freeze!"

I looked over my shoulder and laughed. "There's a pig on the front step. A really big one."

"Bah! You and your jokes, you're naughty just like your father!"

She walked around the other side of the table and yelped.

Piggy greeted her with several grunts.

"Santa Madonna! It's a pig!" *(Holy mother of God!)*

"I *told* you!"

Piggy pushed against my legs but I held my ground, so he moved to the right and tried to squeeze past.

"No! Don't let him in – stand there while I get a towel!"

Piggy was determined to enter and complained loudly every time I blocked him.

Grandma brandished a tea towel. "Shoo! Shoo!"

She flicked it towards him in a futile attempt to push him back outside. Piggy had decided he was coming into the warm room and was using his large body to his advantage to push past me and Grandma.

"Noor, stop laughing and help me! Go around the table and block him!"

With tears streaming down my face and gasping for breath, I moved to the other side of the table and blocked him. With me on one side of the table and Grandma on the other, Piggy had little room to move and very reluctantly backed out.

"Hurry, grab a towel and shoo him with me," Grandma called over her shoulder as she barricaded the doorway with her body and inch by inch, made Piggy retreat.

I tried. I tried really hard to stop laughing and help her but all I could manage was to lean weakly on the table clutching my stomach.

"Close the door and wait for me inside," she ordered from the courtyard. "I'm going to call Vico."

I drew in several breaths. "The landlord?" I managed to splutter. "What for?"

"It's *his* pig!" Grandma answered without looking at me.

Staring into Piggy's eyes, she shooed him back out into the courtyard, completely ignoring his grunted complaints.

I closed the door but decided to wait outside with Piggy while Grandma went to call Vico. It was my first time seeing a pig and I might not see him again.

Piggy stood close and stared at me, and I could have sworn there was a glint of mischief and amusement in his eyes.

I WAS STILL CHUCKLING when I set off on the short walk to the newsagent. Across the road from me, Vico's large black dog, and small white and brown one of no identifiable breed, were heading to Grandma's house. Not knowing their names, I had christened the big one Jack and little one Luke. While Vico's cows, and apparently also a pig, lived in the stall in the courtyard in front of Grandma's house, he lived in another house close by with the dogs. Jack and Luke often walked between the two places on their own, giving humans a wide berth or freezing with their tail tucked between their legs. It broke my heart that they were so afraid of humans, but I was determined to show them not all humans are dangerous or cruel. It had always been my childhood dream to have a cat and dog. I had managed to convince my parents to get me a cat, but unfortunately not a dog. So I made the best of it and befriended everyone else's dog instead.

They saw me and froze for a moment before their tails gave the smallest wag and they moved a little closer.

"Hello little sweet peas," I spoke softly to avoid scaring them. "I've got a surprise for you."

Very slowly, I pulled out the bread rolls stuffed with ham that I had smuggled out and gently put them on the grass near Jack and Luke, careful not to get too close and scare them away like last time.

They could smell the ham and their tails started wagging a little more, but they waited for me to step back before devouring their treats. I eyed their visible rib cages under their short fur and frowned. They were too skinny for my liking. They sniffed in the grass for a little more food and looked up at me, tails wagging more energetically.

I smiled and stood up. "See you at lunch tomorrow."

Grandma wasn't happy about me leaving food for them outside the front door, but I wasn't about to stop. She was worried Vico would be upset by me feeding his dogs, so I made a point of asking-yet not asking the first time I saw him with them.

"You don't mind if I feed your doggies, do you? I love dogs."

What could the man say? He mumbled something and walked away which I interpreted as permission granted. Jack and Luke quickly learned to turn up by the door around noon, and I would step outside and feed them bits of ham, salami and bread that I had saved for them. Sometimes I managed to sneak them some pieces of cheese too which they seemed to love.

I blew them a kiss, (we weren't at the patting stage of our blossoming friendship yet) and walked on to the newsagent.

The man behind the counter was tall, thin, balding and always wore a sweater that made him look more like a professor than a newsagent.

"Hello again," he smiled. "Let me guess – you want the latest issue of Topolino?"

I grinned and nodded. "Do you have any copies left of the Christmas special?"

"You're in luck. I only have two more copies of the Christmas ones but plenty of the weekly one. Are you getting both?"

"Um... " I pulled out my wallet and looked inside. "Just the Christmas special please."

I really need to get to the bank soon and sort out my ATM card. For some reason I couldn't understand, I hadn't been able to withdraw money from any ATM I had tried so far.

"Do you read these?" He asked curiously. "I only ask because they are meant for children but you're 18."

Blushing, I stammered the first thought that popped into my head. "Um - they are for… um, my younger sister… "

"Oh, how sweet," he commented with a smile. "I'm sure she will love them."

I paid and still blushing, left rather quickly. No need to mention that my younger sister was 16 years old and these cartoon comics were for me. We all have an inner child in us, and I occasionally like to indulge mine.

CHAPTER 10

THE BLACK VIRGIN COVERED
IN SNOW

The morning light trickles through the wooden shutters and dances on my eyelids when the church bells start to ring. One, two, three, four, five, six, seven. I burrow under my blankets, savouring the warmth while I still can. The mornings have been getting colder, and for the last couple of days, the water has frozen in the pipes. When it eventually thaws enough to come out of the tap, it's as cold as ice and washing my hands and face carries a risk of frostbite.

I listen to grandma's careful steps down the slippery metal stairs, the familiar sound of the large iron key turning all four locks (installed after she was burgled) and quietly lighting the fire in the wood stove. Grabbing the hot water bottle from the bottom of my bed, I hugged it to my chest and opened the thin doors separating my room from the kitchen/meal/living room area.

"Good morning nonna."

"Oh good, you're up. I was just about to come wake you."

"Is the water frozen again?"

"Yes, it was a cold night. But you should be happy – it will snow soon."

I rub my half closed eyes with the back of my hand. "How do you know?"

"If it gets cold enough to freeze the water in the pipes, it means snow is coming."

Unconvinced, I wash my face using the lukewarm water in the hot water bottle.

Everyone keeps telling me it will snow soon, but so far it's only been snowing in the higher parts of the mountains. I desperately wanted a white Christmas like the ones from my childhood. There is something magical about waking up to a hushed, white world but I had a bad feeling it wasn't going to snow this year.

By the time I'm finished, grandma has warmed the milk in a saucepan and poured it into two mugs for us. I take out the jar of honey and put a spoonful in each one, then fetch the biscuits she likes to eat for breakfast. It doesn't take long to clean up and I get dressed in my usual look –hand knitted wool jumpers (thanks grandma), jeans, and a couple of pairs of wool socks so thick they increase my foot size, but keep my toes from freezing and falling off.

Grandma is already standing by the door, wrapping herself in various wool shawls before putting on her coat and outdoor shoes with jerky movements. She's been stressed about our shopping trip since last night because we need to shop at *both* of the village bakeries, which also double as small grocery stores. Roberta's bakery is closest and where grandma buys all her bread, cheese and ham. The other bakery is run by three siblings; two sisters and their brother.

"Hurry up!" Grandma said, fidgeting with her coat buttons. "Your uncle will be here soon and we still need to get the bread. We'll have to hurry with the rest of the shopping and be back before Angela picks you up - "

"Relax, we have plenty of time," I tell her, struggling to pull my boots over the socks.

"But we have to buy the bread and be back before Francesco gets here. What if Roberta's shop is busy? There could be a queue then your uncle will wonder where we are –"

"What queue?" I cut her off before she could work herself into a frenzied state. "The village has, like, three people! I bet you she won't have even opened the store yet."

Grandma pursed her lips and clutched her shopping basket. "Hmm. Maybe."

I sighed and tugged on my other boot. "Why couldn't we just get everything we need from the other bakery? We're going there anyway to pick up the cake."

"I need some vegetables from there too. Roberta's shop just doesn't have a large variety of vegetables… " She said almost mournfully.

"So why rush now? We could have just got everything from there."

"I can't do that! What if Roberta finds out that I shopped at the other bakery?"

I shrugged. "So what? We needed a cake, she doesn't make cakes and the three siblings do."

Grandma shakes her head in a firm no. "You don't understand. I've been shopping at Roberta' store longer than you have been alive. She might be offended if she finds out I buy from another store as well."

"But it doesn't make sense to have to carry food all the way to the butcher's shop, the other bakery and back home."

"True… Alright, I'll just buy our usual amount of bread from Roberta, then she won't be suspicious and we can get everything else we need from the siblings' bakery."

I rolled my eyes but didn't argue further. In a way, she was right but it was very difficult for me to understand small village politics because for the past eight years we have been shopping for food in a large corporate supermarket. Even when we did go to the local market, there was no sense of loyalty to the store holders because they might change from week to week and we didn't know them personally. They weren't our neighbours and we didn't see them at community events.

As I had predicted, Roberta's store wasn't open yet but

Grandma refused to acknowledge my 'I told you so' look. We were the first, and only customers, and finished so promptly we had to wait several minutes for Uncle Francesco. He dropped us off in the village centre and left to get ready for work, while we waited for the butcher and the bank to open. I left Grandma at the butcher's counter and lined up to talk to a bank teller. My Visa card still wasn't working, and I hadn't been able to withdraw cash from any of the ATMs around Italy. By the time the teller had checked the card, assured me there was nothing wrong with it and the money was visible on her screen, Grandma was waiting outside looking anxious.

"So? Did they fix it?"

I shook my head. "They told me to try a main bank in Biella."

"Never mind, we'll sort it out another time. Now let's go get that cake - I ordered apple and pear with chestnuts. Make sure you carry it carefully when you go to Angela's."

Nodding, I shoved the worry aside and followed her to the bakery by the river.

I COULD SMELL FRESHLY BAKED bread and pastries from around the corner. I pushed open the heavy wooden door, making the bell jingle and the other customers turn to stare.

"Buongiorno," Grandma greeted them.

"Buongiorno," the old ladies answered, their straw baskets full of purchases.

It was smaller than Roberta's shop but looked more like my idea of a village bakery/grocery store. A refrigerated glass cabinet stuffed full of cheeses and cured meats took up most of the room, with the fresh fruits and vegetables displayed in baskets in front of it.

Grandma collected the cake she had ordered, chose some fruit and vegetables and smiled indulgently when she caught me staring at my favourite childhood treats - Kinder fetta al latte (a soft and fluffy chocolate sponge stuffed with a creamy, milky filling) and Kinder Pingui (similar concept except it's covered by a layer of chocolate and must be kept in the fridge, so it's a bit more like an ice-cream). She didn't normally buy sweets but as it was almost Christmas, she made an exception and bought me a packet of Kinder fetta al latte *and* Kinder Pingui.

I ripped open a Kinder Pingui as soon as I walked through the door.

"You're having chocolate now? But it's still morning!"

"You have biscuits for breakfast," I pointed out in between bites.

"*Vitamin* biscuits."

"Oh, come on nonna, they don't sell this in Australia so I have to make up for lost time."

"You'll spoil your lunch! Angela will think you don't like her cooking," she worried.

I laughed. "No danger of that, this is a tiny snack."

"Your teeth will rot and fall out," she threatened but I was too old to fall for that again.

"I'll take my chances," I grinned.

Hoping to distract her from my chocolate snack, I asked her to remind me how Angela was related to us, even though I knew perfectly well that Angela's mother Emilia was grandma's first cousin. Like grandma, she had moved to Piemonte from Veneto when she got married and had lived here ever since. The rest of the family remained in Veneto so Grandma maintained close ties with Emilia and her only child Angela. Being of a similar age, Angela and my dad had played together as children, and my sister and I had played with Angela's children, and so we maintained the bonds of kinship alive through several generations.

Grandma was still talking about her relatives from Veneto when we heard a knock on the door. Instead of Angela, her children Vittoria and Pietro walked in with a tall, lean young man trailing in behind them.

"Anna, this is my boyfriend Berto," Vittoria introduced him with an adoring look.

"Piacere," he said, shaking our hands. *(Pleased to meet you.)*

Pietro, with a long-suffering look on his face, made polite conversation with Grandma as his sister and her boyfriend could barely stop staring at each other. I cunningly disguised a laugh into a cough and talked to him and Grandma. Angela was busy preparing lunch and they had come a little earlier than planned so we could go for a walk in Biella before the meal. Seizing the opportunity, I asked if we had enough time to stop by the bank there and explained the trouble I had been having with my card. Vittoria overheard me and quickly organized for their father Lorenzo to meet us at the bank where he had worked before retiring. He had several contacts there and she assured me someone would be able to work out what the problem was. Relieved to get some help, I promised Grandma to be back in time for dinner and almost walked out without the cake she had ordered especially for today's lunch.

VITTORIA AND BERTO sat in the back, holding hands and gazing deeply into each other's eyes. Pietro motioned for me to sit in the passenger seat.

"Thank goodness you can keep me company today. Those two are in a world of their own," he said, rolling his eyes. "She stole my best friend and I have become the third wheel and chaufer."

Laughing, I settled into the car seat and tried to answer his questions about Australian flora and fauna – a topic he knew more about since he was completing a PhD in Biology. A short drive later, we parked the car and walked over to the bank. His sister and her Romeo walked behind us, still holding hands and whispering in each other's ears. Lorenzo was waiting for us outside the bank and after an affectionate greeting, he took me inside to talk to his former colleagues. After almost half an hour of investigating the problem, they worked out that the security pin on my card hadn't been entered correctly and without it I couldn't access my money. My only option was to have a new card issued by my bank in Australia, but it could take weeks to arrive and it would be difficult to do without me being present. Sniffling, I wiped away tears of frustration, thanked Lorenzo for his offer to lend me money and assured him I still had some left. Besides, Dad had already told Grandma and Uncle Francesco he would wire money to them if I needed more, but I was determined to fund this trip on my own. I had three hundred euros left and I was sure I could make them last another couple of months. I just had to spend carefully.

There was nothing else we could do so we headed to their family home for lunch. Angela had been cooking all morning and if anything could cheer me up now, it was her food.

THE HOUSE STOOD PROUDLY on the corner of a somewhat busy road near the town centre of Biella. Guarded by large iron gates and a stone wall, the three storey building with stair-cases cloaked in shadows and adjoining gardens were the perfect setting for ghost tales. Nothing amused Pietro more than telling his younger cousins about the creepy sounds coming from the empty apartments on the ground and top floor. I knew better than to believe his stories now, but I still walked up those stairs pretty quickly.

Angela was waiting for us at the door. As usual, her grey hair was elegantly arranged and the pearl necklace just visible above the top of the apron.

"My dear, how wonderful to see you!" she said, embracing me tightly.

I heard her sniffling and patted her back.

"Have I told you that I have a box full of all the birthday and Christmas cards you sent us?"

"Really?" She pulled back and smiled at me. "You kept them all?"

I grinned. "Of course. It was always a nice surprise to receive your cards."

"Mum, stop crying, she's not going back for weeks!" Pietro told her, taking off his coat and scarf. "Let's have lunch, I'm starving."

Angela wiped her tears on the apron. "You're right, let's make the most of our time together now. Everything is ready. Go through to the dining room and I'll start serving the food."

"Let's have an aperitif to celebrate," Pietro announced, popping open a bottle of spumante.

"A toast, to welcome Noor back," Angela suggested. "And to hope the rest of the family can make it back too. I would love to see your sister again!"

Lorenzo raised his glass. "Welcome back Noor."

"Cheers!"

"Chin chin!"

I blinked away tears and sipped the sparkling white wine. "Yum!"

"Do you like it?" Lorenzo asked. "It's a regional specialty called Asti. Some more?"

"Better not or I'll fall asleep at the table," I said, chuckling. "I can smell your baking Angela."

She smiled warmly. "I made croissants with home-made plum jam from our trees. I hope you're hungry because it's a proper meal today with antipasti, primo and secondo."

Lunch was a leisurely affair and lasted several hours. Good food, good company and enjoyable conversation made the time fly. At some point, a shy tortoise shell called Puzzi jumped up onto Lorenzo's lap to be patted. I showed them pictures from my tour around Italy and Angela, a very keen gardener, showed me her book on Australian native flora. Pietro on the other hand was more interested in Australia's large range of poisonous animals. Vittoria and Berto would occasionally stop gazing at each other long enough to join the conversation while Pietro rolled his eyes in their direction.

"Si sono presi una bella cottura," he muttered, making me laugh.

His description was quite accurate – they were consumed by the fever of love.

"Noor, do you want to see snow in Oropa?" Pietro asked. "It snowed last night, not much but enough for a snowball fight."

"Oh yes please!"

"I don't think it's a good idea to go to Oropa today," Angela said. "It gets dark early and it's a dangerous road to drive."

"We'll be fine!" Pietro answered.

"Your mother is right," Lorenzo said, calmly stroking the purring Puzzi. "Besides, we haven't put on snow chains on the car tyres yet."

"Oh, come on Dad! It barely snowed and we'll drive slowly," Pietro said. "If we leave right now, we can come back before dark."

"We'll be careful," Vittoria promised.

Her parents looked unconvinced but outnumbered, they reluctantly agree to let us go.

After several more hugs from Angela, and a few more tears slipping out, we left for Oropa and I could barely contain my excitement.

I knew it had only snowed a few centimetres but I didn't care. Any snow, however little, was better than no snow at all.

"Here, sit in the front with me," Pietro invited.

Vittoria and Berto climbed into the back and resumed their hand holding. Pietro and I looked at each other and laughed.

"Stop laughing at us," Berto complained. "You'll understand when you fall in love!"

"Fine, fine, we'll stop laughing at you," Pietro answered, giving me a conspiratorial wink while I smothered a laugh.

The small car was better suited to driving through Biella

than up narrow, windy, and sometimes slippery, mountain roads.

To their credit, Berto and Vittoria tried to make conversation in between exchanging loving glances and holding hands.

"Have you been to the Sanctuary of Oropa before?" Berto asked curiously.

"Oh yeah, many times when I was younger. Nonna used to take us and make us drink water from that fountain with the big ladles."

"Really? How come?" Berto asked.

I snorted a laugh. "She thought the holy water would turn us into well behaved children."

Pietro laughed. "Obviously, it doesn't work. Well, you got lucky. Doesn't look like we'll get much snow this year, but it's been snowing in Oropa for the past couple of days."

I couldn't wipe the grin off my face. One of the things I had missed most during my time in Australia was snow. Oropa was very close to Pollone, but being at a higher altitude of 1159 meters above sea level compared to Pollone's 630 meters, it always snowed there first.

"Noor, do you know the legend of the Sanctuary?" Vittoria asked.

"Um… well, no, not really. I know Grandma comes here every year on a pilgrimage and lights candles."

"Lots of people do," said Berto. "They've been doing it since the 17th century to thank the Black Madonna for protecting Biella from the plague."

"Huh. But why is she black? This is the only place I've seen a black Madonna."

"That's an even older legend. Apparently Saint Eusebius brought the statue back with him from Jerusalem in the 4th century," Berto explained.

"Some people believe it was carved by Saint Luke," Pietro added. "We can't stay long because I promised your Grandma we'd take you back in time for dinner."

"I don't think she'll care if I'm late for dinner. Not if we tell her we came to the sanctuary."

"True, true," Pietro chuckled and parked the car.

It was breathtaking. The serenity of the mountains, the dignity of the tall pine trees around the Sanctuary, the echo of the wind gently drifting between the columns and the purity of the white snow gave the place an ethereal feeling.

It was my first time seeing the Sanctuary in winter and I was transfixed.

Splat!

Gasping, I whirled around.

Pietro was laughing hysterically, while Vittoria and Berto ran for cover behind the columns.

"Alright, who was it? Own up!"

Splat!

Pietro grinned and aimed again.

I ducked just in time and grabbed a handful of snow. "You'll pay for that!"

Trying to turn soft snow into a weapon while avoiding Pietro's onslaught was very difficult.

When did he have time to make so many? I thought, running in a jig zag pattern.

I needed to get close enough to throw my mushy ball, but stay out of range from his.

Vittoria and Berto were safe behind the columns, emerging to attack only when Pietro and I were too busy fighting each other.

Pietro made snowballs with lightning speed. I was completely out of practice, but what I lacked in technique I made up for with enthusiasm. We had to stop and put on serious faces every time a pilgrim or nun walked past, but we would quickly dissolve into a fit of giggles and resume as soon as we were alone again.

We played like children until it was too dark to see and we

were all shivering with cold. So much for the promise to Angela that we would come down the mountain before dark…

"Make sure you dust off all the snow," Vittoria instructed. "Otherwise it will melt in the car and make your clothes wet and cold."

"Yes, and your grandmother will know that instead of praying to the Madonna you were playing in the snow," Pietro sniggered.

"You started it!" I responded indignantly. "Besides, you are all older than me and should set an example. I'll tell Grandma it was your fault."

An empty threat and we all knew it. I was very happy because even though I had been gone for a long time and we had grown up apart, they had welcomed me back with open arms. It was good to be home.

CHAPTER 11
A VERY MERRY CHRISTMAS
TO ALL

I n the week leading up to Christmas, Grandma took me for a walk around the village to see the nativity scenes on display. In Italy, a nativity scene is a very elaborate affair and it is called Preseppio. The stars of the show are there – Mary, baby Jesus, Joseph and the three wise kings – along with a whole cast of supporting characters, from the baker to the wine barrel maker. The quirkiest preseppio was definitely the one on the common land near Grandma's house. Baby dolls dressed as the Holy Family, shepherds, milkmaids, bakers etc. took over the lawn with their alpine style village year after year, much to the delight of the local children.

Creating the preseppio was my favourite part of Christmas. Every year we watched with wide eyes as Dad created a magical mountain landscape, complete with a waterfall and river. When we became old enough to help, it was our job to scrunch up old newspaper to form the mountain shape and cut pieces of sticky tape for him. The figurines, however, were off limit. He had inherited some antique ones from family members, others he had bought, and each was carefully wrapped in cotton wads to protect it from damage. It was very exciting watching them be unwrapped, not knowing which one of our old friends would appear next. It was even more exciting sneaking a few pieces off the display when Dad wasn't looking and playing with them. The trick was to return them before he noticed they were missing, bonus points if we managed to sneak off several pieces at the same time.

"Put on another jumper and pair of socks," Grandma insisted.

"I already have *two* jumpers and pairs of socks on!"

"You'll freeze in those jeans."

"Here, use this thick scarf," she said, wrapping it several times around my neck.

We were struggling to zip up my coat over the bulk of the jumpers when we heard the gravel being crunched under car tyres.

"Hurry up with the coat Grandma!"

She yanked the zip and managed to move it up. "Do you have the keys? And a flashlight?"

"Yes, and yes." I kissed her cheek. "Don't wait up, I don't know what time I'll be back."

Grandma adjusted my scarf and kissed me goodnight before she let me walk out the door.

Gigi was waiting in the car with the heater running, even though he was wearing enough layers for an excursion to Siberia.

"Are you ready Noor?" he asked with a wide grin.

I nodded enthusiastically and buckled my seatbelt.

"How long have you been doing this?" I asked curiously.

"Several years now," he answered, looking straight ahead to navigate the narrow and curvy cobbled road. "It's become a bit of a tradition."

"Do all Alpini soldiers do this?"

"No, just the retired ones. We all belong to local groups of former servicemen and on Christmas Eve, each group goes to a local church that is having midnight mass, and we prepare

Vin Brûlê, hot chocolate, boiled sausages with polenta and pannetone for the people to have after the service."

"We're making all that tonight? I don't know how to make polenta… "

Gigi laughed. He was one of those people who was almost always in a happy mood.

"Not us, we're in charge of the best bit – the wine," he chuckled. "It's good you agreed to come. We need all the help we can get to serve the food and drinks."

"Happy to help," I said, smiling happily.

"The best part is on Christmas day. Some of us dress up as Santa and take toys to the local children whose families are struggling financially."

"I like this tradition."

"Me too," he grinned.

IT DIDN'T TAKE LONG to arrive at the sweet looking village lit up by Christmas lights. The former Alpini servicemen had commandeered the school gymnasium and split it in sections. The rest of our team, a very merry and rosy cheeked bunch who may or may not have already sampled the wine, was already there. Laughing, singing and joking, they filled a pot with red wine.

"Hooo, you're having too much fun over there!" A man from the polenta and sausage making station yelled out. "Have you been sampling the wine?" he asked with a grin.

"Quality control," one of the men from our team yelled out, making the rest of us laugh.

They filled the pot right to the top. It was large enough for me to sit in.

"How much wine is that?" I asked incredulously.

"45 litres," one of them answered. His thick white beard, twinkling eyes and rounded belly reminded me strongly of Santa Claus. "Then we add sugar and spices and boil it."

Gigi sniggered. "Then we add something special at the end."

"What?"

"You'll see."

The men began emptying packet after packet of sugar.

"Do you think 10 kilos will be enough?" Someone asked.

"Yes, we don't want it too sweet. Pass the spices."

"Wait, let Noor take a picture first."

I leaned over the very large cake bowl and snapped a photo of the colourful mix.

Grunting with effort, they lifted the pot onto a portable gas burner and lit it. Someone had brought snacks to share while we waited for the wine to boil.

"What are the spices?" I asked Gigi, munching on a biscuit. "I recognise star anise and orange peel, but what's the rest?"

"Don't worry about that now," Gigi waved his hand. "Watch this bit - the secret ingredient that makes it extra special."

One of the men pulled out a couple of large bottles of Grappa (a grape based pomace brandy that contains between 35 to 60% alcohol), and poured them into the bubbling pot.

I gasped. "You add Grappa?! Won't people get drunk?"

The servicemen around me laughed like naughty schoolboys.

"There is little alcohol left by the time we finish with it," Santa Clause man explained. "We burn it off."

Carefully, he lit a match and held it just above the wine.

Tall flames erupted out of the pot.

Gasping, I jumped back. Santa Clause man had managed to pull his hand away just in time.

"Relax," Gigi chuckled. "We know what we're doing."

I watched the flames get lower and lower until they merged with the rich red wine. The most enticing aroma drifted from the pot and filled the gymnasium.

"And now, we try it!" Gigi slapped me on the back and pushed me forward.

They gathered around the pot and began ladling out cups of wine, perhaps a little too generously, and wishing each other a Merry Christmas.

I took a sip and my eyes widened. The spices danced on my tongue and warmed my blood.

"Well?" Santa Clause man asked. "What do you think?"

"I love it! *hiccup* "

Laughter erupted from the group.

"Good, but you can't have more," said Gigi. "We need you sober to help ladle it out."

I laughed heartily and followed them out of the gymnasium where they had set up a couple of tables with cups. One of the other teams had prepared a giant pot of liquid chocolate.

"Here," Gigi pressed a steaming cup of hot chocolate into my hands. "This will help sober you up. Your cheeks and nose are as red as a drunk!"

"I'm not drunk!" I protested feebly while grabbing the cup.

Smooth and rich, I finished the melted chocolate in no time and licked the sides of the cup to get every last bit.

"Can I have more?" I asked Gigi hopefully.

Laughing, he pointed to my face. "You're covered in chocolate!"

Slightly embarrassed, I wiped my mouth with a hanky and grinned. "It was delicious!"

"If there's any left after we have served people, then you can have some more. I doubt it though, usually it finishes pretty quick. Here, take this - " he handed me a ladle. "One ladle per person, but don't pour it until they are in front of you or the wine gets cold."

"Wait – where are you going?"

"I'm going to help them serve hot chocolate. It's always very popular and we need to work quickly before it cools.

Just shout out if you need anything, and the others will be around to help."

"But... but – you mean, I'm on my own with the wine?"

"Yep, leaving you in charge. Don't worry, I'll be close by," Gigi said with a cheerful wave.

"Don't drink it all on your own," Santa Clause man sniggered, walking past carrying cups and napkins.

"When does the mass finish?" I asked the Alpini at the next table.

"Soon. When the bells ring at midnight, the priest will lead a procession down to the manger and say a prayer, then people will line up for the hot drinks."

"It's beautiful," the man next to him said. "They have a real donkey and, the Virgin Mary and Joseph with baby Jesus make their way to the stable."

I looked in the direction of the 'stable'. It was a wooden shelter with hay scattered on the bottom, complete with a primitive looking wooden crib.

"Are Mary and Joseph really going to sit in there?"

"Yes but not for long or they'll freeze in their thin costumes. We'll take them some wine to warm them up. Unstack your cups so you can quickly grab them – like this."

When I finished, there was nothing for me to do but try to keep warm while we waited. My toes had already gone numb and I was shivering under my many layers of clothes. I didn't know the name of the village of where we were, but I guessed it was a little higher than Pollone because there was a layer of fresh, soft, white snow on the ground.

The church bells rang, sending the Alpini into a flurry of last minute preparations. I looked up at the dark sky dotted with twinkling stars. It was one of those cliché moments that seem like something out of a movie – a starry sky, bright white snow and Church bells ringing. If it was a Christmas movie, Frank Sinatra would be serenading us in the background.

The priest led the procession, followed by a tall, bearded

young man leading a donkey with a pretty young woman sitting side-saddle and clutching a doll. They were accompanied by a shepherd with live sheep and children dressed as angels. Carefully carrying their candles, the congregation followed the Holy Family and their entourage to the makeshift wooden hut. The priest took his time praying but I wasn't paying much attention because Gigi had signalled to start ladling the wine into cups. In what seemed like seconds, there was a long line of shivering people in front of my table. I yanked off my gloves so I could work faster, filling cup after cup.

"Buon Natale e felice anno nuovo," I repeated over and over again. *(Merry Christmas and happy New Year.)*

There is something special about Christmas, it seems to bring out the best in people. Despite the cold, and having to wait in line in the cold, no one was grumpy or complained. Children behaved themselves and people wished each other well for the New Year. It felt quite magical and I was very grateful to be part of this wonderful tradition.

I worked quickly but the line wasn't getting any smaller. There must have been a few hundred people of all ages, or at least it felt like it. It didn't take long before the jarring clank of metal on metal told me the enormous pot was empty.

"Gigi," I called out. "I'm out of wine. Is there any more?"

"No, we've run out of everything!"

Even that didn't seem to upset the people lined up in front of me, although I suspect that some of them were returning for a second helping.

I was exhausted and chilled to the bone, but very happy. It was one of the most magical Christmas Eves I have ever experienced.

By the time I arrived back at Grandma's house it was well past three in the morning. There is nothing quite like stepping into a deliciously warm room with a cheerfully crackling fire when it's cold outside. Grandma had put a large log in the wood stove to keep the fire burning until I came home, and put a hot water bottle under the blankets on my bed. Smiling, I hugged the hot water bottle and almost instantly fell asleep.

It was the delicious smells from the kitchen that woke me. It took a while before I managed to get dressed and opened the doors to the other room. Grandma, busy preparing a feast at the table, looked up and smiled.

"Ah, I thought you would sleep through lunch. What time did you get back last night?"

"*Very* late," I answered, reaching into the fridge for one of my Kinder snacks.

"Should you be eating chocolate for breakfast?"

"Ish Chrishtmash," I mumbled through a full mouth.

The familiar sound of gravel being crushed under car tyres in the courtyard surprised us.

Grandma looked at the clock. "Francesco's early. The food's not ready yet."

The door burst open and my Uncle stepped carrying large, colourfully wrapped parcels.

"Merry Christmas everybody!"

"Merry Christmas," we echoed back.

"So many gifts! Who are they all for?" Grandma asked.

"You and Noor of course, who else?"

"Can we open them now?" I asked.

"We're about to eat," Grandma objected.

"Oh come on, let's open them now. The food's not ready yet anyway," said Uncle Francesco.

Throwing her hands up, Grandma huffed. "Like small children who can't wait. Fine, we'll open them now."

I ran into my room and pulled out the presents hidden under the bed. My parents had sent gifts and typical souvenirs for all our relatives which I had carefully wrapped with Christmas wrapping paper.

"Merry Christmas Uncle Francesco," I said, handing him

his parcels. "I hope you like your presents – Dad picked them."

"Merry Christmas nonna," I said, giving her a hug and kiss along with her gift.

Grandma seemed to be more sentimental than usual and I could have sworn her eyes seemed moist.

"Here," she whispered, shoving money into my hand. "This is for when you go stay with your friend Lisa. Try to make it last."

I looked at the crisp fifty euro note and swallowed a lump in my throat. I hadn't told her how worried I was about my money running out, especially with my upcoming trip to Brescia. I didn't need to. She knew and was helping me even though all she had was a small, aged pension.

CHAPTER 12
VAL D'AOSTA - SO MUCH MORE THAN A SKIING DESTINATION

"Tell your father where you're going today," Grandma said as she cleared away the breakfast things from the table. Raising her voice a little louder, "I hardly get to see her. Day trips to Turin, skiing in Aosta, lunches, dinners… "

"That's not true!" I objected loudly. "I spend every day with you, and I've only been on a few day trips."

"*You* went skiing?" Mum interjected from the other side of the world.

When they called me, which was almost every morning, they put me on loudspeaker and huddled together around the phone. It made for very entertaining conversations with everyone talking over each other.

"Uncle Francesco went skiing," I corrected. "I sat in the café next to the fireplace, reading and drinking hot chocolate until it was time to go home."

"Ha!" Dad snorted. "So where are you going today?"

"Gigi and Sara are taking me to Val d'Aosta."

"Tell Gigi to show you the barracks in Aosta. I did my military service there and my Dad carved the doors for the barracks."

"Wow, that's so cool! How come you never told me before?"

"You never asked. Check if the doors are still there and take a photo for me. If you don't have time to see it today, maybe Francesco can show you another day."

"I'll try to see it today. We're going to see the Fortress of Bard, and if we have time we'll visit the city of Aosta too."

"You'll probably be late for dinner," Grandma grumbled, half listening to the conversation.

I rolled my eyes. Grandma's insistence on eating dinner at 6 pm sharp made day trips a little difficult, especially as she refused to eat her own dinner until I came home.

Dad, an ancient history enthusiast like me, spent the rest of the conversation giving me a history lesson on Aosta, starting from the first inhabitants of the region, the Celts and Ligures, telling me how the Romans had trouble conquering the north of Italy, and how 400 soldiers at Fort Bard stopped Napolean's 40,000 strong army from invading in 1800. Vastly outnumbered, these soldiers held the pass for two weeks before Napolean (in a foul and vindictive mood at having his invasion and domination plans thwarted) ordered that the fort be razed to the ground. Luckily, the fort was rebuilt by Charles Albert of Savoy in 1830, and I was thrilled to have the opportunity to visit.

Gigi and Sara arrived while dad was explaining how Aosta and Piemonte used to be one region. After a quick goodbye to my family and promising Grandma I would be in time for dinner, we set off for the one hour drive. Gigi and Sara made good use of the drive to plan our next day trip to Aosta, for the annual woodcarving fair of Sant' Orso. Lucky for me, it occurred *after* my trip to Brescia, so I could still spend a week with Lisa and enjoy the local fair! They were still describing all the incredible things they had seen at previous fairs when Fort Bard came into view.

Strategically situated on top of a rocky hill, in a narrow gorge above the Dora Baltea river, the Fort dominates the entrance to the Aosta Valley.

· · ·

I was glad I wore my comfortable walking shoes. The plan was to walk through the beautiful medieval village of Bard and up the path to the Fort, which seemed a long way away from where Gigi had parked the car.

"We're lucky it didn't snow overnight," said Sara.

"I was hoping for a white Christmas," I responded glumly.

"No, this is much better," Gigi contradicted. "It's a nightmare travelling when the roads are covered in snow and ice."

"You can appreciate the beauty of the snow because you don't have to live with the difficulties it brings," Sara added.

I didn't argue back. They were probably right that I didn't appreciate the difficulties of living with snow, but after surviving several heat-waves in Australia, I was relishing a colder climate.

"How long is the walk to the Fort?" I changed the subject.

"Not sure, maybe an hour?" Gigi answered. "This is our first time visiting it too. It's lucky you came this year because it just opened as the Museum of the Alps."

"They've been doing restoration works for years," Sarah added. "Ah, here's the path up to the fortress."

"Wow, it's so pretty!" I pulled out my camera and started taking pictures of the narrow, cobbled street with stone houses on either side. Everywhere I looked, a preseppio was on display.

"Ooooh! Look at that one!" I rushed over and began taking close up photos.

Each stone step had a part of the nativity scene and village, and it was best appreciated by taking a step back to see it as a complete picture.

"Sara, Noor, you have to see this one." Gigi was standing next to a stone water trough with a big grin on his face.

I peered down and gasped. "An underwater preseppio? I've never seen one before."

"You're going to love this one," said Sarah, steering me

towards the other side of the narrow street where a bunch of corn cobs had been carefully dressed as the Holy Family.

Laughing, I took several photos.

"Have you ever seen one like this before?" I asked Sara.

"No, but they eat a lot of Polenta here too, so it makes sense they would have a preseppio out of corn cobs."

"Aaah!" Gigi exclaimed, waving his arm. "I've found a traditional preseppio of Val d'Aosta."

"They're famous for wood and stone carving in this area," Sara explained over her shoulder.

I stopped in front of the display and stared. Some of the figurines had a carved wooden face with a stone carved into the shape of the body, and some had a face carved out of stone with a wooden body.

"How do they merge stone and wood like that?! It looks seamless."

"It's a speciality of the area," Sara told me. "You'll see more of this style at the fair."

"I hate to hurry us," Gigi interjected, "but we need to keep moving up to the Fort if you want to have lunch at a reasonable hour."

"That means he's getting hungry," Sara rolled her eyes at me.

"Breakfast was a long time ago," Gigi said and grinned.

Chuckling, I took a few more photos and followed them up the very steep path to the Fort.

THE WALK up to the Fort was quiet. Gigi was leading the way, Sara was admiring the view and I was too busy huffing and puffing, sweating and swearing under my breath to make conversation.

"Come on you too," Gigi called out from higher up the path. "We're almost at the top."

When I eventually reached the top, I had to admit it was

worth the climb. From up here, I could see the village of Bard below and an eagle view of the valley. The scenery was breathtaking and the Fort, imposing. Beautifully restored, it proudly guarded Aosta once more.

I lost track time wandering in and out of the different exhibits. At some point I lost track of Sara and Gigi too and we had all ended up in different parts of the museum. The contingency plan was to meet back at the gates but Sara found me first and Gigi burst into the room soon after.

"There you are! I've been looking for you for ages. Aren't you hungry? It's well past lunchtime."

"We were about to come looking for you," Sara told her husband. "I know of a really good restaurant where they serve authentic local cuisine."

Gigi looked worried. "We're going to have trouble finding places that are open so soon after Christmas. Maybe we should brought a picnic with us… "

"Don't worry, I've already checked and they *are* open today. You just drive and follow my directions," Sara told him.

It was lucky for us Sara had organized today's trip. If it was left up to me, I would have either gone hungry or found a street vendor for some food, but this lunch seemed more promising.

We arrived at a small restaurant with quaint wooden furniture and were quickly seated by a friendly waitress. The dining room was mostly empty, which is not surprising considering it was the holiday season and most people were spending it with their families.

"What would you like to have?" Sara asked me while Gigi browsed through his menu.

"Um… don't know… everything sounds delicious."

Sara turned to the waitress patiently standing by. "Can you recommend some dishes? We would like to try some typical local foods."

"Ah, then you must try our 'zuppa valpellinese', and for desert 'brunet' with 'pere martin sec', which is very nice with coffee."

The glance I threw Sara's way was slightly alarmed. I had no idea what the waitress had just recommended and if the baffled look on Sara's face was anything to go by, neither did she.

"Can you tell us what 'zuppa val'pellinese' is?" Gigi asked curiously.

The waitress smiled and nodded, her dark ponytail bouncing with the movement. "Is layers of pan ner cooked in butter, with broccoli and melted fontina cheese between. Is perfect food for cold weather."

"Pan ner?" I asked. "What' black bread?"

"It's a typical bread they make here," Sara told me. "I always buy a loaf when I come up and put slices of it in the freezer. It's delicious."

"For holidays we make it with figs, nuts and raisins," the waitress added. "Cut it, put slice of lard and honey on it. Good food for winter, but for zuppa val'pellinese we use plain pan ner."

"I love the fontina cheese you make here," Gigi told the waitress. "I'll have the zuppa."

"Me too," said Sara.

"I'll have some too," I said. "I've never had a typical dish from Val d'Aosta before."

"What about the dessert? What did you call it?" Sara asked the waitress.

"Brunet with pere martin sec," the waitress repeated.

"I don't know what it is, but it sounds delicious," Gigi said to no one in particular.

"Everyone loves it," the waitress assured us. "Brunet is cake made of amaretti buiscuits and chocolate. You eat it with pears cooked in red wine, with a red wine sauce and some cream. That's the 'pere martin sec' part of the dessert."

"That sounds divine!" Sara said and looked at us. "Shall we order three?"

Gigi and I nodded vigorously.

The waitress smiled. "Take a small piece of cake on your spoon, add pears with sauce and cream on top. That is how you eat it."

The dessert sounded even better than the main meal and luckily for my rumbling stomach, we didn't have to wait long for the food to arrive.

The fontina cheese in the zuppa was perfectly melted and the black bread very filling, but nothing could have possibly compared to the dessert. Every mouthful was a delight and if my stomach wasn't on the verge of exploding, I would have had a second helping.

"What's next on the itinerary Ms Tour Guide?" Gigi teased his wife.

Sara turned to me. "Do you mind if we go for a bit of a drive? There's a cottage nearby where we get our cheese from. It's in the mountains but not far from here, and I'll make sure we have enough time to stop by the barracks on the way home."

"I don't mind," I answered truthfully. I was enjoying every minute of my visit to Aosta.

"We come to Aosta several times a year and buy cheese from Osvaldo's cottage. He makes it himself and sells it straight from his cottage cellars. It's more delicious and cheaper than the ones you buy in the market," Sara explained apologetically.

"Really, I don't mind at all." I gave them both my most reassuring smile. "I love seeing all these different parts of Aosta. What kind of cheese does he make?"

"Typical cheeses of Aosta but also other cheeses we are familiar with," Sara explained.

"They make some cheeses in Aosta that aren't easily available in other parts of Italy. Have you had Toma before?" Gigi asked.

"Is it like the Tomini cheese?"

"No, it's not a soft, fresh cheese like Tomini. It's aged and has a more smokey flavour," Gigi explained then drained his espresso in one gulp.

"You'll see when we get there," Sara said as she bundled up and checked our table to make sure we hadn't left anything behind. "The cows live in stables next to his cottage, and all the cheese is made from their fresh milk. He lets you taste samples."

I had already eaten more cheese with my lunch than most people do in a week, but I wasn't going to pass up this opportunity. After all, how many times would I get the chance to eat artisan made cheese from cows that are on the property? The milk and cheese doesn't get any fresher than that. Besides, there is something in the mountain grass and herbs where the cows graze that gives their milk such a lovely, rich flavour.

A SHORT DRIVE LATER, Gigi parked the car on the gravel driveway of a mountain cottage. I could hear the cows mooing from their stables as we walked up to the door.

"Ciao Osvaldo," Sara greeted the man who came out to meet us.

Stout, grey haired and with red cheeks, he was the picture of robust health that comes with living in the mountains surrounded by pure air.

"Ciao! You have come for more cheese?"

"Yes, and this time we have brought a friend with us from very far away to try your cheeses. Her father is Piemontese, but they are living in Australia now."

Osvaldo looked at me curiously. "Does she speak Italian?"

"Yes, I do," I answered in Italian and got a smile from him.

He waved his arm towards the door. "Go down to cellar. I have excellent toma you can try."

I didn't need to be told twice and closely followed Gigi and Sara down the dimly lit stone steps. With each step, the temperature dropped and by the last one I was shivering despite my coat and two wool jumpers.

Osvaldo led us into an enormous cellar full of shelves with large and small wheels of cheese in varying stages of maturity. The adjoining cellar was full of small wheels of fresh, soft cheese.

Picking up a large wheel, Osvaldo cut out small pieces and held out his hand. "Try this."

Moving carefully among the full shelves, he picked up several other cheeses, sniffed them and cut out pieces for us to try.

I nibbled everything I was given, trying to make the pieces last. I wanted to buy some as a surprise for Grandma and Uncle Francesco but I couldn't choose. All were delicious.

"We'll take 5 kilos of Fontina, 3 kilos of Toma, and 2 kilo of that one," Sara told Osvaldo.

"So much cheese! Won't it spoil?" I asked curiously.

"No, we keep it in our own cellar and we share some with friends," Gigi answered.

Osvaldo's large knife was barely visible as he quickly cut the pieces, weighed and wrapped them in brown paper.

"Would you like to get anything?" Sara asked me while Osvaldo calculated the costs with a pencil on a piece of paper.

"Yes, I'd like half a kilo of Toma. I think Grandma and Uncle Francesco will like it too."

"Ok and then we'll go straight to the barracks while there is still enough daylight to take a photo," Sara briskly organized me and Gigi.

We paid and carefully packed the cheese in the car.

"We'll be back soon Osvaldo," Sara waved out the window.

"Ciao!" Osvaldo waved goodbye and returned to his Aladdin's cave of cheese.

Lucky man.

I'VE NEVER SEEN barracks before and wasn't sure what to expect, but the white, square building looked very ordinary. A young Alpino was on guard duty outside the locked gates. The small structure he stood in looked like a miniature version of the barracks – plain, white and solid.

Gigi walked right up to him with me trailing nervously behind.

"Hello, I'm an Alpino too. This is my friend's daughter all the way from Australia. Her dad did his military service in this barracks, and her grandfather carved the entrance doors. Can we take a photo of her in your guard post?"

The soldier nodded, moved out of the way and indicated for me to step inside.

"Thank you so much, we'll be quick," Gigi told him before turning to me. "Put your hand up and give a military salute. Your dad will laugh when he sees the photo!"

"Stop talking and take the photo before it gets dark," Sara called out, standing near the car.

Gigi alternated between yelling out instructions on how to give a proper military salute and laughing when I got it wrong. It took me a few tries, much to the amusement of the soldier on duty and Gigi, but I eventually gave a passable salute and the photo was taken.

"Can we get closer to the doors?" Gigi asked the Alpino hopefully.

"No, this is as close as you are allowed. If you stand over here though, you can see the doors fairly clearly through the gate."

Not what I had hoped for, but it would have to do. Activating the zoom function on my cheap camera, I snapped a few shots hoping that one of them wouldn't be blurry.

"Hurry or you'll be late for dinner," Gigi called out with one foot in the car.

I didn't need to be told twice. I thanked the soldier and hopped into the car. If traffic was good, I'd make it back just in time. If I was a few minutes late, I was counting on my gift of cheese to mollify Grandma.

CHAPTER 13
OLD FRIENDS IN A NEW CITY

I spent as much time as possible with Grandma before my trip to Brescia. To try and make up for my upcoming week's absence, I even watched the news with her. Several times a day. Lisa called to finalize the details and organized for her mum Alice to pick me up after work - which saved me the trouble of trying to get there by train, and most likely getting lost along the way.

Grandma fretted about everything. She worried I would get robbed. Then she worried we would have a car accident because it was a two hour drive and there was ice and sludge on the roads. She worried I would get cold and packed some extra wool jumpers and socks. I wasn't to talk to strangers and if I didn't like it there, I could come back early. I hugged her, told her I would miss her and promised to call.

THE DRIVE WAS an excellent opportunity to exchange information. Alice wanted to know news about my parents and sister and what life was like in Australia. While Lisa and I exchanged long letters covered in many brightly coloured stickers, our parents could only talk occasionally on the phone and for short times. International calls were very expensive.

I wanted to know more about their move to Brescia and details on everything I had missed out on since moving. Alice good-naturedly told me about her oldest daughter, Sofie, moving to Belgium to live near their relatives, her youngest son Gabriel focusing on classical studies in his final high school years and her husband Mark's new post as a Vicar. The subject of Lisa's boyfriend was mentioned briefly between pursed lips.

"It's impressive that you can still speak Italian so well. Do you remember much about your life in Italy?" Alice asked.

I grinned. "Lots. I remember spending hours playing in your apartment in Biella, and the mountain village Piedicavallo we would visit during summer."

"Yes, you children loved it there. You would run wild from morning until it was dark, and only come home to eat."

"I remember one year your nieces and nephews came to visit from Belgium, and we all slept over in the church cottage and swam in the river."

"That's right! Lisa is so excited to see you. You two did a great job maintaining your friendship for all these years."

I smiled at her, but I was feeling a little nervous. Would Lisa be the same? Would we still get along like we used to when we were children? What if she had changed and didn't like me any more? Maybe that's why the letters had become less frequent?

Alice's voice snapped me out of my train of thought. "Lisa has planned to take you sight-seeing around Brescia and Lake Garda. She mentioned something about a day trip to Milan?"

"Ah, yes, I'm meeting my cousin there. He's visiting from Germany."

"You girls be careful in Milan," Alice warned in a serious tone. "It's full of pick pockets."

"Don't worry, we'll stick together and look out for each

other," I promised Alice. "Besides, if I do get robbed, I will be having the last laugh – my wallet is practically empty!"

Alice chuckled. "Yes, Lisa is quite safe like that too. It's always like that for students."

I looked out the window as Alice navigated Brescia's brightly lit and noisy streets. After living in a quiet mountain village for several weeks, being in a city was a bit of a shock. It was 10 PM and while the streets of Pollone would be silent and practically deserted, the streets of Brescia were full of people walking and talking loudly.

"Almost there," Alice said. "Do you mind sharing a room with Lisa? Otherwise I can set up a bed for you in the living room."

"No, I don't mind sharing if Lisa doesn't."

"Try not to stay up all night talking," Alice said with a mock stern look. "She has school in the morning."

"No promises," I chuckled.

Alice stopped the car in front of a large church veiled in shadows. The garden and iron fence separated the church from the city, preventing the glaring street lights from dispelling the darkness.

"I hope you don't mind a late dinner," Alice said apologetically. "We don't really have set mealtimes. It depends a lot on my work schedule and when everyone is home. We tend to wait until everyone is home so we can eat together."

I ignored my rumbling stomach which had been trained by Grandma to eat at 6 PM sharp and grabbed my bags. "Don't worry about me, I'm pretty flexible."

Alice closed the iron gate and led the way down the side of the building to a small side door. It was dark and we were depending on the dim light from the street's lamp-post.

"Our apartment is on the terrace, so we'll have to go up three flights of stairs. Can you manage with your bag? Otherwise, leave it here and I'll send Gabriel to get it," Alice said as she fumbled with the keys.

"It's okay, I can manage."

I followed Alice up the large stone stairs, occasionally mumbling a response but not focusing on the conversation. My stomach had butterflies and I was feeling quite anxious. Maybe this had not been a good idea. After all, I had not seen Lisa in eight years and now I was going to spend almost a week with her? What if we didn't get along? Pollone was over two hours away. It's not like I could just hop on a train and make my way easily back to Grandma's house.

Alice opened the door to the apartment and a warm, welcoming light flooded the landing.

"Ragazzi, we're here!" Alice called out. "Lisa, Gabriel, hurry up - I've brought Noor." *(Guys)*

My heart thudded against my rib cage. Two lean figures emerged from the shadows of the corridor and strolled into the entrance where Alice and I stood.

Lisa smiled and hugged me. "It's good to see you."

"You too," I said, returning the hug.

Gabriel smiled shyly and gave me a quick hug. "Welcome to Brescia."

"Thank you. Gosh, you've grown so much taller than me!" I paused. "Do you remember how we used to make you play 'tea parties' with us?"

Gabriel chuckled and rubbed the back of his neck. "Yeah, you and Lisa used to make me play with your dolls too."

Lisa and I looked at each other and laughed.

"It's wonderful to see you children together again! It's too bad your sister Marina isn't here too," Alice said. "Never mind, maybe she'll come next time. I'll go prepare dinner and call you when it's ready. Lisa, why don't you take Noor to your room and help her settle in? Gabriel, where's your father?"

"In his office. I'll go call him," Gabriel volunteered and walked away.

I looked at Lisa again. The same hazel eyes, chestnut hair and slightly bronzed skin tone. The only difference was that she had grown taller than me and with her slim figure, she looked very elegant.

I supressed a sigh. *My younger sister is taller than me. Lisa is taller than me. Even Gabriel is taller than me and he is almost three years younger!*

"My room is this way," Lisa smiled and reached for my bag.

I nodded and followed her down the corridor into a large room with a bunk bed at one end, a large wardrobe with clothes overflowing onto the floor and a desk covered with burning incense sticks. Posters and pictures covered the walls and on the other side of the room, across from the bunk beds, glass double doors opened up onto the largest terrace I had ever seen.

"Which bed would you like?" Lisa indicated to the top and bottom bunk.

"Um, can I sleep on the bottom one please? I'm a bit scared of heights."

Lisa nodded and moved her pyjamas to the top bunk. We smiled at each other awkwardly.

I hate awkward silences and always feel a need to fill them, usually by saying the first thing that comes to mind.

"Would it be alright if I checked my email on your computer? I'm organizing our day trip to Milan with my cousin."

"Yes, sure. You can use it anytime. We keep the computer in Dad's home office, next to the kitchen. I'll show you where it is later."

"Thank you for coming with me to Milan," I said gratefully. "I would have gotten lost going on my own."

Lisa grinned. "No problem. I love travelling and I've been to Milan before so I can be your tour guide."

Another awkward silence filled the room as we both stared at each other with smiles plastered on our faces. It had never been like this before. We used to talk and laugh for hours…

"I'm sorry I haven't been writing to you as often," Lisa broke the silence. "I'm in my final year of high school and studying for exams."

"It's okay," I said quickly. "It was the same for me in my final year. Besides, with email these days it's much easier and faster than writing a letter and having to go to the post office to mail it."

"I know, but it's not the same as a handwritten letter... Actually, I kept all the letters you sent me."

"Really?!"

Lisa got up, rummaged through the wardrobe and pulled out a pretty box. She opened it and showed a stack of letters full of childish scribbles and a more elegant form from recent years.

Taking a deep breath, I blinked away the tears that had formed.

She didn't forget me, I sniffed. *Even though we didn't write as much, she kept them all and took them with her when she moved.*

When I regained my composure, I looked up and smiled at my oldest friend.

"I kept all your letters too," I told her.

What I did not tell her was that I had re-read her letters over and over while I cried during my first year in Australia. I could barely speak English, the children at school teased me for my accent and school lunches, and I struggled to make friends. Those letters had been a great comfort during a very difficult transition to a new country.

We grinned at each other and just like that, any lingering awkwardness was gone. The chatter flowed non-stop and barely halted when Gabriel poked his head into the room to call us for dinner. We joined Alice and Mark at the table for a very late dinner.

"Noor, we are so pleased could come and spend time with us," Mark said in his gentle way. He had always been a kind and gentle soul, much like his son Gabriel.

"Thank you for letting me stay," I smiled happily. "I've been looking forward to this visit for a long time."

"I'm afraid dinner is a little haphazard," Alice said in her practically perfect English. "We threw together whatever we could find in the fridge and cupboards."

"It looks delicious," I reassured her. "And it's lovely that you wait until you're all together before eating."

"Tell us about your parents and sister, and life in Australia," Mark said, also in English. "We never forgot our dear friends, and I hope we can see them again one day."

"Shall I speak in Italian or English?" I asked my meal companions.

"English," Mark smiled. "We can all understand it and it is good practice for the children."

I almost laughed. The children certainly did not need to practice their English. Unlike many people in Italy, Lisa and her siblings spoke near perfect English thanks to their mother's tutoring. Lisa was actually fluent in several other languages besides English and Italian; including Flemish, French, Portuguese and Spanish. Gabriel was learning ancient Greek. I on the other hand, was only fluent in English, Italian and was learning Spanish at university. I could understand and speak Lebanese, but could not read or write it anymore. Compared to this multi-lingual family, I felt a little uneducated.

We took our time over dinner catching up on years of separation. When we finally made it to bed, Lisa and I turned the lights off but stayed up giggling and talking in hushed voices until Alice came in and ordered us to sleep.

I had a feeling that it was going to be a great week.

CHAPTER 14
BRESCIA, THE CITY OF MIGRANTS

I woke up early the next morning to have breakfast with Lisa and Gabriel. They both had to go to school and their parents had to go to work, so they gave me the keys to the house and told me to make myself comfortable. Everyone would be back around lunchtime as the schools finished at one o'clock.

"There are lots of books in my room if you want to read something," Lisa told me, shoving things into her backpack. "We're in the city's centre so you can walk around and have a look at the shops and restaurants. And there are Roman ruins close by. If you get lost, just ask them to point you in the direction of the church."

"Where's the closest public phone?" I asked. "I want to call my parents."

"Actually, there's an international call centre just across the road. They sell phone cards that are cheaper than elsewhere and you get a lot more time. I use it all the time when I want to make an international call."

"Really? I haven't seen these international call centres in Italy before," I said.

"It's because Brescia has so many migrants from all over

the world. Much more than other parts of Italy," Gabriel chimed in.

"Okay, I'll try it. Thanks."

"If you're interested, you could come to school with me one day and see what it's like," Lisa invited. "I can't take you today because I have an exam."

"Yeah, I would love to." I had only gone to primary school in Italy, and had no idea what a typical day in Italian high school would be like.

Alice rushed through the room, grabbing her handbag and yanking on a coat. "Will you be all right on your own? Did someone give you a copy of the house keys? We'll be back by lunch."

"Stop worrying mum," Lisa told her. "We already gave her a set of keys and she can take care of herself."

"I am so sorry to leave you alone this morning, Noor. I have to work but I will take you on a tour of the city after lunch," Alice promised, snatching her keys off the table and practically running out the door. "Have a great day kids, see you at lunch."

"Make yourself at home." Lisa kissed my cheek goodbye and walked out with Gabriel.

"See you soon!" I smiled and waved until they were out of sight down the staircase.

Mark had already left for the day and the house suddenly seemed very quiet. I cleaned up in the kitchen and went into the next room to check my email. Mark's study/home office was full of serious looking books, which I suppose is a requirement for a Vicar and theologian. On the way back to Lisa's room I passed by the living room and stopped to look around. Brightly coloured rugs, which Alice had already told me were handmade in Morocco, covered the polished wooden floor. Cheerful paintings and family vacation photos covered the walls. I loved everything about Lisa's family home. Books, hundreds of them, and many, many potted plants filled the large living space. Just about every room of the house had a number of potted plants, and there was one that I recognised from my childhood. I don't know how this tree survived living indoors all these years, or the move, but it had grown bigger and flourished. It was so tall now that its branches touched the top of the ceiling. Alice had always loved her plants, and had clearly not left them behind when they moved.

"Hello old friend," I gently stroked the trunk of the tree that was probably older than I was.

This is what my house will look like one day, I thought to myself. Warm, inviting, comfortable and dotted with interesting souvenirs from my travels around the world.

Smiling, I walked back towards Lisa's room. Down the corridor were the two bedrooms used by her parents and brother, as well as a family bathroom. We were lucky enough to have our own smaller bathroom right to next to Lisa's bedroom. I felt very comfortable in Lisa's room and bathroom – she was just as messy as me!

I picked up one of her Spanish language books and settled on a comfy bean bag.

I might as well use my time productively and practice Spanish.

I flicked through the pages, picked up another book and flicked through it. When I glanced at the clock, only half an hour had passed.

It was so quiet and empty without the family's cheerful chatter or music playing in the background.

Tick Tock, Tick Tock, went the cuckoo clock.

The empty house seemed to amplify the sound.

I wrote letters to my friends in Australia.

Tick Tock, Tick Tock, Tick Tock.

It was too quiet. I could dimly hear the noise from the street below through the closed windows, and it was a lot more inviting than sitting in silence.

I might as well try the call centre across the street.

I carefully locked the apartment door and walked down the three flights of stairs to the side door that opened into the garden. The noise hit me as soon as I opened the door. I stood still for a moment, too stunned to move. This was very different to the quiet life in Pollone and the suburbs of Melbourne. This was city living and it was a little bit intimidating.

Grimacing, I crossed the large, leafy garden and let myself out through the iron gate. I could see the call centre across the road, and walked over quickly. When the thick glass doors closed behind me and dulled the street noise, I sighed in relief.

"Hello, I would like to make a call to Australia."

The young man behind the counter smiled. "Australia is a bit expensive to call."

"I know. I'll buy the 20 Euro credit note please," I said, handing the money over. "I haven't used to call centre before. Do I just go into one of the booths and dial?"

"Yes, is soundproof inside and you take as long you want. If you have trouble connecting to call, wave to me and I help."

"Thank you very much," I said, accepting the card.

As I walked over to an empty phone booth, the door to the adjacent booth opened and a couple of men emerged speaking in Russian. Lisa had told me there were many Russians in Brescia, as well as Bangladeshi. I was curious to know if moving to Italy had been as difficult for them and the young man behind the counter, as it had been for my family to move to Australia and learn English. I almost asked, but changed my mind in case they found it rude and nosy.

I followed the lengthy instructions on the call card and waited impatiently for the connection to be made.

"Hello?"

"Dad, it's me."

"Saide," Dad shouted excitedly. "Noor is on the phone!"

A second later Mum's voice came through as they both tried to talk to me at the same time.

"How are you? How are Mark and Alice?"

"Are you having fun with Lisa? It's very quiet in the house without you."

"And neater," Mum added with a laugh. "If I tidy a room, it stays that way."

"Enjoy having a neat house while you can," I said, laughing with her. "I can't make any promises for when I get back. How did you know I was already in Brescia?"

"Of course we knew," Dad answered. "We talked to your Grandma. We're going to call Alice and Mark when they are home so we can chat with them too."

"They told me to say hello, and that they miss you."

"Alice was such a good friend to me while we lived in Italy," Mum said sadly. "I miss her."

"Are you having fun with Lisa?" Dad repeated.

"She's at school this morning, so I will see her at lunch."

"Don't worry about calling us. International calls are expensive. We'll call you, so save your money for souvenirs," Mum told me.

"It's okay, I found a call centre right across from their house and I think it's cheaper than the call cards I was buying."

"Okay, enjoy yourself and don't stay out too late," Dad instructed.

"No alcohol, no drugs, no boys," Mum said with a note of panic in her voice.

I rolled my eyes at the colourful poster stuck on the wall in front of me. "Yes Mum."

"We love you," my parents said and hung up.

I listened to the annoying *beep beep beep* of the line before putting the receiver back. I was missing my family more than I had thought I would. I had wanted to come on this trip for so many years, but now that I was here I kept thinking about my family - including my little fur ball cat Susu (affection-ately dubbed SquishyBoo).

I still had credit left so I made another call, this time to a German mobile number. My mum's cousin, who had been a childhood playmate in Lebanon, was studying in Germany and we had arranged to meet up in Milan during my stay in Brescia. I hadn't seen him in many years and since we were both in Europe at the same time, it was the perfect opportunity for a family reunion.

"Hello?" a young man's voice said in German.

"Christian? Is that you? It's Noor."

"My little cousin!" Chris said happily. "Where are you calling from? It's a strange number."

"I'm in a call centre. I got your email but I thought it would be quicker to organize tomorrow by phone. I'm sorry I couldn't come to Milan today. My friend Lisa had school in the morning and I don't think I can get to Milan by train on my own. Not without getting lost along the way."

Chris laughed. "That's ok. I am going to use today to shop for work clothes. All the major fashion houses are having sales so it's a great time to prepare my professional wardrobe."

"I thought you were still a uni student?"

"Yes, but I have a prestigious internship and I want to make a good impression. I'm looking forward to seeing you tomorrow little cousin."

"Me too! Where should we meet?"

"I'll give you my hotel address, and when you arrive ask the concierge at the lobby to call my room. That way we don't risk getting lost among crowds of people."

"Ok, I have pen and paper."

I wrote down the address and promised I would be there as early as I could.

Relieved at having organized tomorrow's excursion, I hung up and walked out of the call centre. I didn't want to go too far from the Church in case I got lost, so I kept it in my sight and walked down the street directly in front of it.

It seemed to be one of the main streets and was full of shops selling everything you could possibly need. My shopping funds were very limited, but thankfully window-shopping was free. I walked in and out of several shops - expensive boutique stores with elegant but unfriendly Italian shop assistants, and cheaper clothing and handbag stores run by Chinese immigrants who could barely speak Italian and no English. It was a surreal experience for me.

The Italy I had left behind eight years ago did not have so many migrants. Especially in Pollone where everyone who lived there was a local, and their families had lived there for generations before them. My sister and I had been considered foreigners because our mum is Lebanese. The only other 'foreigners' in Pollone had been a family from the island of Sardinia, and a young family of refugees from the former Yugoslavia. I will admit that it was a bit of a shock to see so many people from other countries now living in Italy. Not a bad thing, just unexpected. Brescia was beginning to feel a little like Melbourne to me, and I was starting to feel at home in an unknown city.

By the time I finished exploring the street it was almost lunchtime so I made my way back to the apartment, just as Lisa, Gabriel and Alice were arriving.

"Perfect timing," Alice said cheerfully. "Mark is already home and we can have lunch soon. After that, we can go visit the piazza and have a look at the little markets."

"That sounds great," I said, as we all followed her up the stairs like little ducklings.

"How did your exam go?" I asked Lisa, shrugging out of my coat and hanging it up.

She made a face. "I hate exams. At least it's over now and we can enjoy the afternoon. I told my boyfriend Kobi to meet us at the piazza so I can introduce you. Tonight I will take you to see the Bangladeshi circolo he goes to."

"Circolo? What's that?"

"A lot of migrants have them," Lisa explained. "It's like a members club and you can only go in if you know a club member."

"Do you mean a club like a nightclub?"

Gabriel laughed. "No, it's nothing like that. They just get together after work and have a drink at the bar, maybe some food and play chess or pool."

"They are very friendly and welcoming," Lisa told me. "I've been there many times with Kobi and have taken Gabriel too. He liked it." She turned to her brother. "Do you want to come with us tonight?"

"Thanks, but I have an exam to prepare for," Gabriel said glumly.

"Study for it another time," Lisa told him cheerfully. "Besides, you're always studying. I'm sure you don't need to study anymore and know everything back to front."

Gabriel rolled his eyes at her and led the way to the kitchen. "You'll find any excuse to study less and now that Noor is here, I bet you won't study at all."

"Lisa knows she has to prepare for her exams, and I am sure that Noor will understand," Alice said sternly, as she quickly chopped vegetables at the kitchen bench.

Mark was already there and had set the table so we all helped to prepare lunch. It's amazing how efficient people can work when they are hungry and impatient to eat.

"I can't wait for you to meet Kobi!" Lisa said.

Mark and Gabriel busied themselves with the food on their plate.

"Now that Noor is here, you won't have much time to spend with Kobi," Alice told her daughter.

Lisa frowned. "Why not? We can all hang out together."

"Noor came all the way from Australia to see *you*, not your boyfriend."

Gabriel and Mark were concentrating very hard on chewing the food.

Lisa and Alice frowned at each other.

I copied Gabriel and Mark, focusing on the plate in front of me.

"I think you will like him Noor," Lisa said in a cheerful tone that was a little forced. "He came to Italy from Bangladesh on his own 10 years ago and has had a really interesting life. He is so cool and worldly," she gushed.

"That's the problem," Alice said flatly. "He is too old for you."

"Oh Mum! Not that again! It's just a number and numbers don't mean anything when it comes to love," Lisa argued.

"You're 19 and he's 30 years old!" Alice snapped.

My jaw dropped and I quickly tried to close it before Lisa noticed.

"So? He is mature and I don't like the stupid boys my age. They are all so *immature*."

Please don't involve me in your argument, I desperately prayed.

"Don't you think he is too old for her, Noor?" Alice asked in a tone that clearly expected me to agree with her.

"No she doesn't," Lisa answered. "Do you Noor?"

I sat like a rabbit caught in headlights, mouth opening and closing with no sound coming out. What could I say? I was shocked at the huge age difference and secretly agreed with Alice, but Lisa was my friend. There was no way I could side with her mother. At least not publicly.

"Let's all calm down and enjoy our time together," Mark spoke up. "And it's not fair to involve our guest in your ongoing argument."

Neither Lisa or Alice looked happy, but complied with his request.

I was extremely grateful to have escaped having to answer, and even more thankful that the lunch finished soon after.

ALICE, Lisa and I walked to the nearby open air market that seemed to be run by migrants from Eastern Europe, Bangladesh and even Peru. Lisa and Alice seemed to be in a much better mood, talking with the stall owners and laughing together. That is, until Kobi turned up.

He wasn't like anything I had imagined and I could see why Lisa thought he was cool. Taller than most Bangladeshis I had seen, he had long dreadlocks, a leather jacket and walked with a swagger and a big grin like someone who knows he is handsome.

"You must be Noor." He held out his hand and I shook it. "Lisa has talked about you so much, it's nice to finally meet you."

"You too," I lied.

So far almost everything I knew about him, I had discovered from the argument between Lisa and her mum.

"Hi Alice," Kobi greeted his potential mother-in-law cheerfully.

"Hello Kobi," Alice said in a neutral tone then busied herself looking through the stalls.

Lisa was holding onto his arm and beaming at him with a love-struck look on her face that made me want to laugh and yet feel guilty like I was intruding on an intimate moment. Stifling my laugher, I looked away and pretended I was interested in the second-hand clothes. Out of the corner of my eye, I could see the couple holding hands and whispering to each other. They seemed to be having a disagreement about something if Lisa's pout was anything to go by.

"He *is* too old for her, isn't he?" Alice muttered to me.

I gulped and gave a non-committal "Mmmm."

Kobi and Lisa walked into our line of sight. Alice continued rummaging through the clothes.

"I know you have plans for this afternoon, so I just came to say hi," said Kobi. "Lisa will bring you to the circolo tonight and you can meet my friends."

"Stay with us," Lisa pleaded. "You can help me show Noor the city."

"No, you should spend time with your friend. I'll see you tonight."

Alice looked up. "We can all have dinner together one night while Noor is here."

Kobi nodded and waved goodbye, walking through the crowd with a confident swagger that I found myself envying.

"What will you girls see this afternoon?"

"I was thinking I would take Noor around the city to see the roman ruins and maybe the museum too, if we have time."

"Yes, good idea. I will have dinner ready by 7 so try to be back by then."

"Do you need help getting dinner ready?" I asked Alice.

"If you feel up to it, sure. We can all cook together," Alice answered with a smile.

We left Alice at the market and went around the city exploring.

LISA MADE A WONDERFUL GUIDE. She knew so much about Brescia's fascinating history – such as it was founded over 3000 years ago and pre-dates Roman times, and had been conquered by various powers over the centuries. Now, it had developed into an industrial powerhouse. I love history and Lisa loves being a tour guide so the afternoon passed by splendidly. We stopped for a energizing cup of fruit tea in a very hippie looking café, where we sat on stuffed cushions surrounded by posters with feminist slogans. It was a refreshing break before we headed off to the local museum to view some more ancient Roman ruins, which the city was apparently full of.

Dinner was a cheerful event, interrupted towards the end by a phone call from my parents. They were still chatting on the phone to Alice and Mark when Lisa and I left to meet Kobi at the Bangladeshi circolo.

The club was close to Lisa's home, or at least it seemed that way to me. Distance is a relative thing and it always seems to be much shorter when travelling with enjoyable company. The club was nestled among other shops, with many of its patrons flowing out onto the sidewalk.

Lisa and I were the only women there. The young men stopped their conversations to stare at us as we walked past. Completely ignoring them, Lisa walked straight to the back of the room where Kobi was sitting with friends.

"Welcome," Kobi greeted me.

His friends jumped up and indicated to the seats they had just vacated. "Please, sit here."

"It's ok, you don't need to give us your seats," Lisa told them, but they kept gesturing for us to sit and wouldn't stop until we did.

"Can I get you a drink?" one of them asked me.

I blushed and stammered. "I don't drink alcohol."

Kobi said something to them in Bengali and they moved away from the table with a reluctant look on their faces. Lisa looked annoyed.

"They don't need to do that," she muttered. "We're living in modern times!"

"Did you enjoy your afternoon?" Kobi asked politely.

"Yes, thank you. I think I saw most of Brescia and we even had time to visit the museum." I tried to answer cheerfully to hide the hint of nervousness in my voice.

His friends, and most of the men in the club, kept glancing in our direction.

"Why aren't there any Bangladeshi women here? I only see young men."

"Because most of the Bangladeshi migrants are men," Lisa explained. "They come to work in Italy so they can send money back to Bangladesh to support their families. It's why Kobi came to Italy by himself when he was 20. It was so difficult for him! He had to learn Italian on his own and try to find work, all while experiencing racism."

Kobi shrugged and smiled.

"Tell her how you arrived in Italy," Lisa urged.

"I paid some smugglers to get me in through Eastern Europe. They hid us in the bottom of trucks and smuggled us across the border that way."

My jaw dropped. I had heard of stories like this but had never actually met someone who had experienced it first-hand. My difficulties in migrating to a different country, and having to learn a new culture and language, seemed very trivial compared to the obstacles Kobi had faced.

"Is all your family still in Bangladesh?" I asked him.

He nodded and took a sip of his cold beer. "Yes. The money I earn working in a factory here can support my family."

I could see why Lisa admired him. He worked hard to provide for his parents and younger siblings, and did it all on his own in a foreign country.

"Kobi is an Italian citizen now but he still experiences a lot of racism," Lisa informed me angrily. "One night, I was walking with him and a policeman came up to me and asked me if I was alright, and if Kobi was harassing me."

"Why?" I asked without thinking.

"Because Kobi has dark skin and some Italians are very racist!" Lisa was getting very worked up but Kobi was silently staring at his beer bottle. "I told him Kobi is an Italian citizen but the police didn't believe me and demanded to see ID."

"How do you know it was because of that? Maybe the policeman thought you were in trouble, seeing a young woman with a man in the dark…"

"No," Lisa cut me off loudly. "I *know* it was because of his skin colour because I walk around with friends at night all the time, and my white male friends have never been stopped when we walk together. Why not? Why not ask for their ID? Why not ask me if I needed help with them? Are only dark men dangerous to women?"

I didn't know what to say. I was half Italian and looked like other Italians, but had received racist remarks by other Italians when I was a child. Some people had even made comments about my olive complexion, even though there were a few people in the village with a darker complexion than me. If it had been so difficult for me being only slightly different, it must have been so much harder for Kobi. Some people are obsessed with focusing on insignificant differences between them and other humans instead of realising how much more they have in common. It's quite sad because they miss out on the wonderful cross-cultural interactions they could have.

Kobi was looking uncomfortable and Lisa looked angry at the injustice of the world, unaware, or not caring, that people were looking at us.

"Would you like to return to live in Bangladesh one day?" I said, changing the subject.

"I don't know," Kobi answered truthfully. "I love Italy. I feel free here, and I can be myself."

I kept the conversation focused on more light hearted topics and was pleased to see both Kobi and Lisa relax. Kobi's friends joined us at the table and they started playing a game of chess. Lisa and I watched them for a while before we had to start heading home.

The walk home took longer than the walk to the club, mostly because Lisa stopped every few meters to greet friends and introduce me. Work and school were over for the day, and even though it was winter, young and older people enjoyed a night walk down the main street. Some stopped to have a warm drink in the cafes that were still open. Others just enjoyed walking up and down the street while chatting with their friends.

Every now and then, a group of young immigrant men (either from Eastern Europe or Bangladesh), would call out to us.

"Hey beautiful, what are your names?"

"Give me your number!"

They always act so brave when standing in a group, but would they be as brave and approach a girl if they were on their own? I highly doubted it.

"Ignore them Noor. They are idiots with nothing better to do than stand around on the street trying to pick up girls."

I ignored their waving arms and whistles and stared ahead as instructed. It seemed to give them a clear idea we were not interested and they would soon stop calling after us.

Except for one guy.

"Girls, come join us for a drink," he smirked.

We kept walking.

"Don't ignore me! It's just one drink, stop being so uptight."

Lisa turned around and gave him a rather stern talking to in very rapid Italian, which may have possibly contained a number of swear words that I shall not repeat. And then came her magnificent exit.

She flipped her hair over her shoulder, gave him the finger and walked away with her chin held high. I gaped after her for a few seconds before gathering my wits and running to catch up. I looked at her furious face and burst out laughing.

"The look –" I gasped, laughing too hard to continue. "The look on his face -"

I doubled over, laughing so hard I accidentally snorted.

Lisa's lips twitched into a smile, her chuckle lengthening into laughter. We laughed so hard tears ran down our faces and our stomachs cramped.

"I bet he wasn't expecting that from you," I finally gasped.

"No, I'm sure he thought he was very cool and we should be flattered to get his attention," Lisa sniggered. "I'm not an object!"

"Well, you certainly taught him a lesson," I said following her up the stairs to the apartment.

"Hmpf! Forget about him. We better get to sleep, we have an early start tomorrow," Lisa said over her shoulder.

Still chuckling, I got ready for bed quickly. If walking down the street from her house was this exciting, exploring Milan with Lisa was sure to be a lot of fun.

CHAPTER 15
MILAN, CITY OF FASHION AND FLEA MARKETS

"**N**oor, wake up," Lisa whispered, shaking my shoulder. "We overslept! It's already 6:45!"

I mumbled something halfway between a curse and that I didn't want to go to Milan.

Lisa laughed quietly and yanked the blankets off me. "Hurry up or we'll miss the train."

Still half asleep, I dragged myself out of bed and stumbled around getting ready. Breakfast was a quick Nutella on toast with a cup of tea, trying not to make too much noise so we wouldn't wake up the rest of the household. I don't know how I managed to get down all the stairs in my sleepy state, but as soon as the cold morning air hit me I was instantly wide awake.

"Good grief," I grumbled, shoving my hands in my pockets. "I can't believe it's so cold."

"It will feel even colder riding the bikes," Lisa informed me.

"What bikes?"

"I already asked Gabriel and he said you can borrow his."

"But – but - I thought we were walking to the train station?"

Lisa shook her head and wheeled out her large, white

bicycle. "No, it takes too long. If we miss this train we'll have to wait an hour for the next one."

"What if we jogged?" I suggested weakly, watching Lisa wheel out an even larger bike and lean it against the iron fence.

"Hmmm, it looks a bit big for you but you'll be ok. Hop on."

"But I can't ride a bike!"

Lisa stopped and turned to stare at me. "What do you mean you can't ride a bike?"

I shrugged. "I always fall off. I've never been able to get the hang of it."

I had long ago come to terms with my clumsiness and embarrassing inability to ride a bicycle, a skill that most children have mastered. I just can't keep my balance and always fall off. After several injuries, I decided that bike riding was not for me and hadn't touched one in years.

Lisa chewed her bottom lip. "Hmpf, I didn't even think to ask if you could ride and it's too late to walk now! You'll just have to sit on the back of my bike."

"What?! Is that even legal?"

"Don't worry, I do this with my friends all the time. Anyway, there's no police at this time of the morning," Lisa told me brightly.

I gulped and helped her put away Gabriel's bike and lock the gate behind us.

"Where will I sit?"

"On the rack behind my seat. Don't get them tangled with mine while I pedal, and you *have* to keep your feet up off the ground. If you get tired, rest them here -" she pointed to the spots she meant. "Or you can dangle them, but keep them off the ground."

I sat on the rack and lifted my feet as instructed. To keep my feet away from the pedals, my knees stuck out in frog position. My muscles were already straining and we hadn't even started the journey. Butterflies stormed in my stomach and I couldn't tell if I was nervous or excited.

Neither of us had helmets and it was still dark and foggy. Part of my brain told me this was a stupid, reckless and dangerous thing to do. The 18-year-old part of my brain said, 'Don't worry, everything will be fine. Lisa knows what she's doing, she's done this before!'

The 18-year-old part of my brain won the argument.

Lisa started pedalling furiously. I clutched onto her jacket and tried not to scream every time a car came close to us. No bike lanes, no pedestrian footpath. We were on the road with the cars, on a foggy winter morning with only the small flashing bike lights to announce our presence.

"Noor, we need to turn right. I need you to indicate to the cars."

We're going to die, I thought, heart thumping madly.

Somehow, the cars saw us and slowed down to let us turn. The part of my brain that wasn't paralysed with fear registered that my body was cold, my leg muscles were shaking, and my fingers were stiff from clutching Lisa's jacket so tightly. I was trying not to think of how close the cars were to us or that we weren't wearing helmets. By now my leg muscles were spasiming so I dangled my legs, careful to keep my feet off the ground.

"WE'RE ALMOST AT THE STATION," Lisa shouted over her shoulder as she peddled frantically towards a large, red brick building.

We screeched to a halt and jumped off, double checked the bike was locked properly and ran to the platform.

It was 7.30 on the dot. There was no sign of the train.

"Damn!" I wheezed, clutching my side. "All that and we still missed it!"

Hardly puffing, Lisa waved her hand and walked up to an elegantly dressed man nearby.

"Excuse me, has the 7.30 train to Milan already left?"

"No, it hasn't arrived yet. It's probably late," he said and rolled his eyes.

So we waited. And waited.

The train finally turned up at 8 am. I didn't have a mobile to call my cousin and tell him we were arriving late and all I could do was hope he would wait at the hotel. Lisa had brought notes to review for her upcoming exam but after quizzing her for about fifteen minutes, we decided to practice speaking English for the rest of the hour. For her English exam, of course.

LUCKILY FOR US, my cousin's hotel was close to the train station so we didn't have far to walk. Even more luckily for me, Lisa was splendid at reading maps and had a great sense of direction. I happily followed her around like a lost puppy.

She stopped in front of thick glass doors and looked at the address I had scribbled on a scrap piece of paper. "Wow! Is your cousin rich?"

"I think his family is well off. Why do you ask?"

"This is a very expensive hotel. Are you sure he's staying here?"

"That's the address he gave me. I'll ask if he's here at the reception desk."

I pushed the heavy glass doors open and walked in, pausing to stare at the large crystal chandelier dangling from the ceiling. Lisa was right. It looked like a *very* expensive hotel. The floor and walls seem to be made out of marble.

"May I help you?" A thin, reedy voice asked from my left.

Startled, I turned to look at the man who had suddenly materialised. Immaculately dressed in a suit, with a vest and tie, he stared at us with raised eyebrows. Even his name tag was shiny.

I couldn't help but become aware of how Lisa and I were dressed – scruffy jeans and worn out runners. Certainly not the kind of clientele he would be accustomed to welcoming in this spotless, grandiose hotel.

"Um, I'm looking for my cousin. His name is Christian and he's staying in room number 52. Could you please let him know we've arrived?"

The concierge looked us up and down, walked to the desk and picked up the phone – all the time watching us with narrowed eyes.

"He must think we're prostitutes your cousin ordered," Lisa hissed in my ear.

"Don't be ridiculous!" I snorted a laugh. "But I don't think he believes Chris is my cousin. I look too poor to be his cousin."

The concierge walked over to us with a frosty smile. "Your *cousin* will be right down. Please wait for him here in the lobby."

Lisa and I stood in the lobby and tried not to touch anything. This kind of luxurious environment was making us feel very out of place and uncomfortable. It didn't help that every now and then the concierge's eyes would glance up from his desk, as though checking we weren't about to start causing trouble.

The elevator dinged softly and the doors slid open to reveal a very well dressed young man pulling a designer brand suitcase behind him.

"There's my little cousin!" The young man called out.

"Chris! I almost didn't recognise you."

"It's been too long my dear," he said, kissing my cheeks hello in the French way.

"This is my friend Lisa."

"Lovely to meet you. If you will give me a moment, I will check out of the hotel and we can begin our adventure for the day."

Chris checked out and the concierge gave us a warm farewell. It was the friendliest he had been to us so far.

"See? I told you he thought we were prostitutes your

cousin ordered." Lisa whispered.

Overhearing her, Chris laughed. "No, no! It's not that at all. I don't think he approves of me much though."

"Why not?" I asked innocently.

"I had a lady friend in my room the other night," Chris told us without batting an eyelid.

"Um, ok then… So, where should we go first?" I said, looking straight ahead.

"I need to store my luggage at the train station first, then we can go wherever you like," Chris told us with a smile.

"Ok. Train station is this way," Lisa said and led the way.

"You look very chic," I complimented him.

"Thank you," he said warmly. "I'm wearing everything from my favourite designer Armani. You won't believe the great deals I got over the weekend."

"I take it your shopping trip in Milan went well?"

"Yes! I bought six Armani business shirts for only €600!"

"What?!" Lisa and I exclaimed at the same time.

Chris mistook our reaction for excitement and continued enthusiastically. "Yes, it's an unbelievable bargain. I made the most of the sales and saved so much money! I bought these gloves, and the scarf I'm wearing, as well as this letter satchel. Isn't it nice?"

Too stunned to speak, I just nodded.

"The things you bought on sale are worth more than my entire wardrobe," Lisa said with wide eyes.

"Mine too," I added.

Chris laughed - an elegant, sophisticated man of the world laugh. "You're still students. When you enter the workforce, you will realise the importance of first impressions. It's very important to look professional if you are trying to impress your boss and clients."

I glanced down at my clothes and a smile twitched my lips. The impression I must have given the concierge was that of a poor relation. Which I was.

I watched him carefully place his suitcase in the locker,

close the door and double check it was locked properly. If he was unlucky enough to have it stolen, there would be a very well dressed thief walking around Milan.

"Where should we go first?" Lisa asked.

"How about an open air market?" I suggested, fished out a piece of paper from my pocket with the address scribbled on. "I read about it on a travel blog. Apparently it's the biggest market in Milan and you can find lots of interesting things and bargains."

Lisa studied her map for a minute and looked up with a smile. "It's just outside the city but should be easy to get there. We just need to catch the subway and then it's a short walk."

Chris smiled and shrugged. "Whatever you want little cousin."

We caught the subway and walked to the place marked on the map.

It was not what I had expected. It was indeed an open air market, but it was enclosed by a wire fence like a prison camp.

"Where have you brought us?" Chris asked with a hint of alarm in his voice.

"Um… Are we at the right place?" I asked Lisa.

"Yes, this is definitely the address."

"The blog said it was a market… "

"I think it's a flea market," Lisa said.

Chris was staring at the market with wide horrified eyes. "We are going to get robbed. Just look at the people in there. They look… not very law abiding."

"We won't get robbed," Lisa told him but she didn't sound very certain.

"*We* look too poor to be robbed but you might, Mr Designer Labels," I said with a laugh.

"That's not funny!" Chris admonished but Lisa started laughing and I couldn't stop.

"Don't worry, we'll protect you," I teased.

"Seriously though," Lisa said, still chuckling a little. "He might actually get targeted by pickpockets. His clothes show that he is well off. I think it's better if he walked between us."

"I have a better idea," Chris told us. "Let's return to the city. There is a lot to explore there."

"But we came all the way here! Let's just look around a little bit," I pleaded.

"No, I don't think it's a good idea. It looks like a dangerous place, and why look for trouble?" Chris tried to convince us.

I looked at Lisa who shrugged. "I think we'll be okay."

"Look at where we are!" Chris said flinging his arms out. "We are in the middle of nowhere, outside of the city, and the subway is several minutes' walk away. No taxis, and no other people or tourists. I'm not even sure this is a real market."

"Come on Chris, where is your sense of adventure?" I asked with a smile.

Chris sighed deeply and shrugged his shoulders in resignation. "Fine, but you two stay close to me so I can protect you. And we will only take a quick look."

Grinning, Lisa and I stationed ourselves on either side of him and entered the market. In hindsight, I shouldn't have relied on the internet blog and done more research. It definitely wasn't a regular market, but more of a flea market full of second-hand items. Anything and everything seemed to be for sale here including used car tyres, toothbrushes out of packets (which I sincerely hoped were not second-hand), used shoes, car bits…

"Ooh, look at these pants!" Lisa paused and picked them up for a better look. "Aren't they nice? And only five euros!"

"Don't touch anything!" Chris told her in English. "You'll catch something."

"Don't be ridiculous," I said, laughing until I spotted a tooth brush that looked used.

Interestingly enough, no one was speaking Italian. We heard Eastern European languages, Bengali, Spanish from

Latin America, and Arabic. It seemed that Lisa and I were the only Italians there.

A delicious smell drifted past my nose and my stomach rumbled. Breakfast seemed like such a long time ago.

"I'm getting hungry," I announced to my companions.

"Me too. They're selling pizza over there." Lisa pointed to a small food stall across the other side of the market.

"I don't think you should eat anything from a food stall," Chris told us. "You don't know what the hygiene standards are like."

"It's only a slice of pizza," I told him. "I'm sure we'll be safe with pizza."

The two young men behind the counter were speaking a language I didn't recognise but I guessed was from Eastern Europe. I was trying to choose a pizza slice when Lisa's elbow made painful contact with my ribs.

"Look – hahaha - look at the sign – hahahaha -"

I read the handwritten sign in Italian and burst out laughing.

"What does it say?" Chris asked curiously.

I translated into English for him:

"WANTED: two waitresses
    Must be 170 cm tall
    Blonde hair preferable
    Must not weigh more than 60 kg
    Large breasts and small waist preferred
    Enquire within"

"IS THIS A JOKE?" Chris asked while we sniggered.

"It must be," I answered, drawing my breath. "They can't possibly be serious."

"Hey Mirko, we found our waitresses!" One of the young men behind the stall called out.

The other one looked at us with a big grin. "No need to apply, you're hired."

"No, no, we're just looking," I stammered, taking a step back.

Lisa waved her hands frantically. "We're not applying, we're just looking at the pizza."

The one who had smiled at us stepped out from behind the stall, still grinning. "Don't be shy! You'd be perfect waitresses."

Lisa and I hurriedly backed away.

"I knew coming here was a bad idea!" Chris muttered.

"I think we've seen enough of the market," I said.

We briskly marched through the mostly male crowd to the exit while pizza boy and his friends from the nearby stalls laughed.

"Come back! We need waitresses!"

I quickened my pace, trying hard not to laugh.

"HAD ENOUGH ADVENTURE FOR THE DAY?" Chris asked with narrowed eyes on the subway ride back to the city.

I grinned sheepishly. "Sorry, I didn't know it was a flea market."

"It's okay," Chris answered while Lisa laughed. "But I will choose the activities for the rest of the day."

"As long as the first activity is to get some lunch," I told him.

"Absolutely," Chris replied. "I shall treat you to lunch and it won't be from a street stall."

Lisa and I looked at each other with raised eyebrows. Lunch was clearly going to be a far more extravagant affair than we were used to.

"Follow me," Chris happily led the way, "I know a great restaurant. You will love it!"

"Noor, we can't afford to eat here!" Lisa hissed in my ear.

"We're in Piazza del Duomo, it's a super expensive area! I don't have much money with me ..."

"I know," I whispered back grimly. "I'll try and talk him into eating somewhere else."

People say honesty is the best policy, so I tried it even though I knew his sense of Lebanese hospitality meant he would offer, and insist on paying.

"Um, Chris... This is a very expensive area and we didn't bring much money. Maybe we could go find a pizzeria nearby?"

Chris looked at us with surprise. "What are you talking about? Lunch is my treat. I thought you knew that?"

"No way!" Lisa protested. "We can't let you pay for us."

"I insist!" Chris argued. "You came all the way to Milan just to see me, and Lisa has been a wonderful tour guide this morning. It's my pleasure to invite you both to lunch."

I could be just as stubborn as him. Chris has always been generous and I knew his offer was genuine, but I have never felt comfortable with people spending their money on me – it made me feel like I was taking advantage of their generosity.

"You came all the way from Germany to see me so I should be treating you to lunch. We'll find a nice pizzeria nearby."

"How often do I get to do something nice for my little cousin? I haven't seen you in years, so I haven't been able to give you Christmas and birthday presents for years. Will you really deprive me of this opportunity?" He asked with a smile.

I narrowed my eyes at him.

"Emotional manipulation doesn't work on me," I lied.

"Just think of it as a Christmas and birthday present," he insisted.

"Fine, but you have no reason to give *me* Christmas and birthday presents so I will pay for my own lunch," Lisa insisted just as stubbornly.

"Hey, wait a minute! I haven't agreed to anything," I protested but no one listened.

"It is my pleasure to invite you to lunch because you have been such a good friend to my little cousin, and you have come all this way with her. Not to mention that you have also been our tour guide this morning." Chris gave Lisa a disarming smile.

I knew when she looked at me helplessly that he had won. She was wavering and so was I because my rumbling stomach said his logic was quite convincing.

"If you refuse to have lunch with me, I shall be very offended," Chris threatened.

I rolled my eyes at him. "You're impossible!"

Chris grinned and put an arm around our shoulders. "It will be a great lunch. This restaurant makes delicious food!"

The restaurant looked more like an art Gallery. A very expensive and exclusive art Gallery. Lisa and I looked at each other in dismay. Everyone in the restaurant was impeccably dressed in luxurious and sophisticated looking clothes. So was Chris, but he was accompanied by two scruffy looking teenagers.

My stomach tightened in apprehension.

We don't belong here, I thought nervously.

A female Asian tourist had entered before us and was waiting to be seated.

A very pompous looking waiter, wearing a crisp white shirt, black vest and blue tie approached the woman and said loftily in Italian. "May I help you?"

The woman answered in nervous English. "Table for one please?"

"I am sorry," the waiter responded in a very non-apologetic tone in Italian. "No English. No free tables, we are full."

Lisa and I looked at each other in disbelief. The restaurant was very clearly half empty, so why was he turning away? She was well-dressed in expensive looking clothes.

"Table for one?" the woman repeated in broken English.

"No," the butler shook his head firmly. "We are full."

She may not have understood Italian but body language is universal. His tone and unfriendly posture were enough for her to understand she wasn't getting a table.

More politely than the butler deserved, the lady bowed and said thank you in Japanese.

I watched her leave with quiet dignity and felt mortified by the politely rude treatment she had received. Was she not dressed elegantly enough for this place? To me she had looked rich enough to lunch there, but what would I know? Maybe it was exclusive for members, or Italians?

What if he doesn't let Chris in because he can't speak Italian? He'll be so upset! Or worse – what if he doesn't let Chris in because he can see Lisa and I are poor? I thought with sudden dread.

"Chris, what if they don't let us in like the lady in front of us?" I asked worriedly.

"Why wouldn't they?" he asked in genuine surprise while the waiter showed the lady to the front door.

"Well, look at us," I said with a sweeping gesture at our little group. "You're so well dressed and we're... not. Maybe they have standards of clothing to eat here?"

Chris laughed but Lisa didn't join in.

"Noor has a point. You saw how he turned away that lady and she is better dressed than us. He might turn you away because you are with us... " Lisa commented looking worried.

"No, don't worry. He can see you are with me and are my guests," Chris told us confidently.

"I don't think he likes foreigners who speak English," I warned. "Better let me or Lisa talk."

Chris shrugged. "Ok, but you two worry for nothing."

The waiter was back and eying us with a little bit of distaste.

"May I help you?"

I gulped and nudged Lisa to talk for us. She was the more confident one out of the two of us. Plus, I will freely admit I can be a bit of a coward sometimes and this waiter made me feel like I was in trouble with the principal.

"Do you have a table for three, please?" Lisa asked politely.

"Ah, yes of course."

"What did he say?" Chris asked us in English and drew the waiter's attention to him.

"Is this gentleman with you?" No English waiter asked.

"Yes, he is my cousin visiting from Germany," I told him.

The waiter sniffed, his beady eyes looking at us up and down. They rested on our scuffed running shoes. "This way," he said after a pause.

He took us to an elegantly set table in the large dining room.

"I can't believe we got in," I whispered to Lisa.

She nodded with wide eyes.

"Here is the menu, and if you need anything at all, don't hesitate to call me," he instructed and moved back to his guard post by the front door.

"Shall we have some wine?" Chris suggested, voice dripping with delight. He was clearly in his element and enjoying the finery.

"How about white wine?" I didn't like it, but I figured it would stain less than red wine on the linen or silk or whatever expensive material the tablecloth seemed to be made out of. I looked at the several forks, spoons, knives and glasses in front of me with dread. What were they all for? Which one was I supposed to use? I had never felt so unsophisticated and uncultured in my life.

Lisa gasped. "The prices are insane!"

"Don't look at that column," Chris ordered sternly. "You just order whatever you want. You are my guest, and you will insult me if you look at prices."

"You'll be bankrupt from this lunch!" Lisa protested.

I was staring at the menu in horror.

Chris laughed heartily. "No I won't, and I absolutely insist you pay no attention to prices and order whatever you like. Now, what should I have? I need you to translate the menu for me."

I translated his options and made some recommendations. While he was distracted trying to order the white wine, mostly by pointing to the menu, Lisa and I had a rapid whispering session.

Chris and the waiter looked at us for assistance in translation.

"Ready to order?" I asked innocently. "We have decided what we want."

It didn't take long for the food to arrive and it smelled delicious, but Chris was eyeing our pasta dishes with narrowed eyes.

"What is that?" he asked.

"Pasta Genovese, you know – the famous pesto," I told him.

"I can see that, but why did you both order pasta? Wait a minute – are you trying to save me money? Is that why you ordered the cheapest thing on the menu?" Chris demanded.

"Of course not!" I lied making my eyes wide and hopefully innocent looking. "We just love pasta! Don't we, Lisa?"

"Yes, and this is my favourite kind of pasta," Lisa played along splendidly.

"Well… alright, as long as it's what you really want… " he said, but seemed unconvinced.

"How is your polenta and rabbit?" I asked to distract him. "Polenta is traditional from my dad's area. We cook the rabbit in red wine."

"It's delicious!" Chris said enthusiastically as he savoured each bite.

The meal was truly delicious. You could tell that the pesto sauce was fresh and hand-made, and the pasta was cooked to perfection. Even the white wine was enjoyable. I made the most of it because I was sure it would be a long time before I could afford to eat in a place like this again.

"I am thoroughly stuffed," I told the others.

"Shall we go for a walk to help us digest?" Lisa asked.

We both grimaced when Chris pulled out his MasterCard and paid for the meal, but knew it would be a waste of time to argue with him about it.

The sun was shining outside and the Piazza in front of the Duomo was full of locals, tourists and plump pigeons.

"I can't wait to see the Duomo!" I said, pulling out my camera.

"The restaurant where we ate had a view of the Duomo," Chris pointed out.

"I was sitting with my back to it."

I was the first to cross the Piazza and arrive in front of the Duomo.

"What's this?!" I demanded, outraged.

The front of the Duomo was covered by a giant poster with a beautifully illustrated scene of what the inside would have looked like during the Renaissance, complete with people in historical dress. Only the top part of the Duomo was visible above the giant poster.

"Oh no," Lisa said. "They're doing restoration works."

"Are you kidding me?? Of all the years to do restoration works, it had to be *this year*?"

"I thought you knew they were doing restoration works," Chris commented sympathetically.

I shook my head sadly and stared at the massive poster positioned in front of the Duomo.

"I guess I better take a picture anyway," I said, my shoulders slumped.

"We can still go inside," Lisa tried to cheer me up.

Chris put on his Gucci sunglasses. "You girls go ahead and look inside. I'm going to enjoy the sun out here."

"We won't be long," I promised.

I followed Lisa and the other tourists inside.

"We should make the sign of the cross with the holy water," Lisa spoke softly.

"Are we even allowed in here? We're both Protestants, not Catholic."

Lisa shrugged. "How will the priest know?"

"Fair point," I grinned.

I walked around slowly to savour the exquisite architecture. The amount of detail was incredible and the workmanship superb. I was still bitterly disappointed that I couldn't see the outside in all of its glory, but at least the inside was still open to the public. It's so easy to lose track of time in ancient buildings. They seem to be slightly apart from the mortal world and not subject to the same tyranny of time.

"We should probably head back," Lisa said.

I nodded and followed her into the sunshine where we found Chris sitting on a bench chatting to a pretty girl.

I looked at Lisa and grinned wickedly.

"Dad," I called out when I was within earshot. "Have you found Mum?"

Chris's jaw dropped. Behind me, Lisa laughed hysterically.

"She is just joking," Chris told the girl who got up to leave. "She is not my daughter, she is my cousin. My cousin, I swear!"

The girl flipped her hair and walked away without looking back. Lisa and I leaned on each other, snorting with laughter.

"It's not funny."

"Then why are you smiling?" I sniggered.

Chris shook his head, his smile widening. "You're still as naughty as you were as a child."

"Where to next?" Lisa asked when she eventually stopped laughing.

"You really need to see the Galleria Vittorio Emanuele II. It's just over there next to the Duomo," Chris told us.

I didn't know what it was but soon found out that it was the most beautiful shopping gallery I had ever seen in my life.

Everything about it was sumptuous and luxurious but also out of our price range so we didn't linger for long.

There was somewhere else I wanted to explore before Chris had to leave for the airport. I love history, and I loved looking at Castles so we made our way to Castle Sforza. The weather was superb and the sun was shining, so after exploring for a while we lay down on the grass in front of the Castle and watched the clouds. Around us young couples were making out shamelessly, and older couples walked by holding hands. I attributed this behaviour, most commonly seen in springtime, to the unusual appearance of the sun at this time of year.

Chris looked at his watch with a frown. "I hate to ruin our fun, but I need to head back to the station. My flight to Germany leaves tonight… "

"Does the train take you to the airport?"

"No, I'm catching a bus from the train station to the airport."

We headed back to the station, catching a tram and walking down a beautiful street that had a special photo exhibit of places around Italy.

"We still have some time and the station is close. How about a gelato?" Lisa suggested, pointing to a little shop on the other side of the street.

"Good idea, and I'll surprise Chris with it."

"I don't think he'll let us pay for it," Lisa said doubtfully.

"That's why we won't tell him," I grinned.

We left Chris looking at the photo exhibit, with some lame made up excuse of wanting to look at something in a shop, and came back with three giant ice cream cones stuffed full of brightly coloured gelato.

"What's this?" Chris asked in surprise when I handed him a giant cone.

"We wanted to thank you for treating us to a lovely lunch," I answered, handing him a cone. "I don't know your favourite flavours so I picked a few for you to try."

"There is no need to thank me!"

"You gave us a delicious lunch so we wanted to give you something nice too," Lisa told him.

"Thank you," Chris accepted graciously. "I'm sure it's delicious."

We walked to the train station in silence, busy licking our ice cream before it melted. The sky was clear and blue, the sun was shining and I was enjoying an ice cream with friends. Life was pretty good.

THE TRAIN STATION was crowded and since Chris couldn't speak Italian, Lisa and I bought his bus ticket to the airport while he retrieved his luggage from storage.

"You don't need to wait with me," Chris told us. "My bus leaves in a few minutes. You should catch your train before it gets dark."

"Don't be silly, we'll see you off properly," I argued.

"We're not in a rush to get home," Lisa added.

The bus driver shouted in Italian and passengers scurried forward towards the bus.

"Chris, quick, they're loading the luggage already!"

We rushed forward to put his suitcase in with the rest.

"I better get on the bus," Chris said with a sad smile. "I don't trust the bus driver not to leave without me."

"Good idea. Everyone else has already gotten on."

"Look after yourself little cousin. I hope we meet again soon." Chris hugged me and then Lisa. "Thank you for being a wonderful tour guide today."

"It was a pleasure meeting you Mr Designer Labels," Lisa said with a smile.

Chris laughed and climbed onto the bus. He found a window seat towards the back and waived at us. We waved back enthusiastically.

Any second now, the bus will drive off and who knows when I will see Chris again? I thought a little sadly. I was determined to keep waving until the bus drove away. It seemed that Chris also intended on waving until his bus left.

We waved, and waved.

The bus engine didn't start.

Chris looked at us with bafflement and shrugged his shoulders.

"It looks like the bus won't be leaving for a while," I said to Lisa. "Should we leave?"

"Our train doesn't leave for a while so we can stay if you like."

Chris was making gestures with his hands.

"I think he's telling us to leave," I said.

"Let's give him a farewell like the movies," Lisa suggested with a cheeky smile.

One of the best things about old friends is that you don't always have to explain everything. Many times your friends will just understand what you mean without a detailed description. This was one of those times.

Grinning, I nodded and we sat down on the train station steps to wait. It was starting to get dark and we could see Chris getting worried that he would be late for the airport.

"How long have we been waiting?" I asked.

"Almost 10 minutes," Lisa said.

The bus engine roared to life and that was our cue.

Chris had resumed his energetic waving as the bus started to pull away.

Lisa and I grinned at each other and pulled out white tissues. We ran alongside the bus, waving tissues and pretending that we were sobbing.

Through the window, we could see Chris laughing and shaking his head. We ran next to the bus until we couldn't keep up. By this point we were breathless with laughter and exertion.

"I guess it's time to head home," I told Lisa.

"Do you mind if we stop by the circolo and see Kobi before heading home?"

"Not at all." Impulsively, I hugged my oldest friend. "Thanks for coming with me today. It made everything so much more fun."

I knew I would always remember our day in Milan with fondness.

CHAPTER 16
BACK TO BRESCIA

Tired from our day trip to Milan, Lisa and I had overslept and were, consequently, running late for school. After barely brushing our hair and shoving some food in our mouths, we bolted down the stairs.

"Just remember, it's all about balance," Lisa said, handing me Gabriel's bike.

"That's what worries me," I responded eying the bike nervously. "My balance is terrible."

"Let's try it. Just ride until the end of the block and turn back," Lisa instructed.

"What if I ruin Gabriel's bike?"

"I'm sure you'll be fine," Lisa said more confidently than I felt.

"Can't we just take the bus to school?"

"This way is quicker," Lisa shattered my hopes.

I reluctantly climbed on the bike and tried to balance. My take off was wobbly and it didn't get better. I managed a few metres (with much swearing involved) before I overbalanced and crashed into the hard, cold iron fence.

"Never mind," Lisa shouted, running to help me off the pavement.

"Go on without me," I told her, peeling myself off the concrete sidewalk. "You'll be late for your exam."

"No, it's okay. We'll take the bus."

"I almost had it," I told her, rubbing my scraped knees. "I just need a bit more practice."

Lisa shook her head. "We don't have time and we have to go on some busy streets. I don't want to risk you being in an accident with a car because we're in a rush."

I blushed. It was incredibly embarrassing not being able to ride a bike, and I felt bad about inconveniencing Lisa. Especially today.

"I'm sorry. I wish I could ride a bike …"

Lisa smiled and pulled me up. "It's okay. It's more comfortable on the bus anyway. We just have to run to catch it on time."

Running. Damn. Something else I was not good at, but I was determined to keep up with Lisa whatever the cost.

"I'm ready," I told her in a confident voice, which was far from the truth.

"Follow me," Lisa instructed and took off swiftly on her long, lean legs.

I sighed and followed, swearing every time my full satchel jabbed my hip bone.

Breathe, I ordered myself. *Don't give up now.*

My lungs were on the verge of exploding. My face was on fire.

Just as I was about to tell Lisa to go on without me, we arrived at the bus stop.

"We've just made it!" Lisa yelled over her shoulder, frantically waving to the bus driver.

Thankfully, the bus driver seemed to be in a good mood and waited for us.

"Ciao Lisa!" A brunette with bouncing curls called out from the back with an enthusiastic wave.

"Ciao Margherita," Lisa waved back.

I followed her to a couple of empty seats near Margherita,

clutching my side and gasping for breath. Lisa on the other hand looked fresh and composed.

"This is my friend Noor from Australia. She's spending the day at school with me."

"Really? Why?" Margherita asked stupefied.

"Curiosity" I wheezed. Margherita and Lisa politely waited for me to catch my breath. "To compare the final year of high school in Italy to Australia."

"Noor is actually a year younger than us," Lisa told her friend. "But the school year in Australia is different so she got pushed up a year and has already finished high school."

"Wow, lucky you! Are you starting University soon?"

"Actually," I puffed, still red in the face. "I just finished my first year."

Lisa pulled out two tickets and validated them in the machine. I took out my wallet to pay her for my fare but she waved the money away.

"It's a free ride," she said with a wink and Margherita laughed.

"What do you mean?"

Margherita leaned in and spoke in a low conspiratorial tone. "It's a trick students use when we are short on money. When you put the ticket in the machine it cuts out a small piece, so we cut a piece of paper to fit the hole and sticky tape it on. That way you can reuse the ticket and the machine validates it."

"Won't you get caught?"

They both shrugged and Lisa answered, "The ticket inspectors are never on this early. Besides, it gets really expensive and we don't always have the money for a bus fare."

Margherita nodded, making her dark curls bounce. "What else can we do? We have to get to school and some days are too cold to ride bicycles or walk."

I nodded sympathetically. It seemed poverty was a rite of passage for students all over the world and it didn't help that Italy was experiencing high unemployment rates and the national economy was struggling. Everyone was struggling to make ends meet. Except politicians. Even if the economy is bad, politicians never seem to struggle like ordinary people do.

The bus dropped us off near the school, which slightly resembled a fort. The large iron gates at the entrance reminded me of a prison. We walked through to the metal barrier, like the kind at train stations where they force people to go through one at a time. On one side, the metal barrier was attached to an office with a big glass window. The two receptionists inside barely glanced at us and continued with their conversation.

Lisa took me to the library and ran off to do her exam. I browsed the bookshelves and wrote in my travel diary until she returned an hour later.

"Did you get there in time?"

"Yeah. Lucky we caught the bus."

"How did you go?"

Lisa grimaced. "I hate exams but at least it's over! Come on, we need to hurry to class."

We jogged through the empty courtyard towards a plain, red brick building. I was a little disappointed with the school architecture. Considering how beautiful architecture is around Italy, I had expected something a little more grandiose.

"Which class do we have first?" I asked curiously.

"Spanish. By the way, I didn't ask the school's permission to bring you along so try not to draw the teacher's attention."

"What?!" I gasped. "Won't we get into trouble?"

Lisa shrugged and retied her ponytail. "I'm sure it will be fine. They probably won't even notice that you're in the class."

"How could they not notice a student they haven't seen before?"

"I don't think they look closely and I'm sure they don't

care," Lisa said with a laugh. "They're not paid enough to care that much about who is and isn't in their classroom."

I absorbed this information with wide eyes. In my all girl catholic high school, we had a roll call at every class and any absence had to be explained to the teacher with a signed note from our parents.

Lisa began climbing an outdoor staircase.

"Hurry, the class has already started," she called out over her shoulder.

The level of noise coming from the classroom sounded more like an out of control party than a Spanish lesson. And I definitely couldn't hear any Spanish being spoken.

The teacher had her back turned and was writing grammar exercises on the blackboard. The students were socialising. The only two empty seats next to each other were, of course, in the front row. No chance of going unnoticed now. The teacher finished writing, put down the chalk and turned to face the classroom. Her dark brown eyes immediately spotted me.

"You weren't here a minute ago. Who is this?" She asked Lisa in Spanish.

"Ah, sorry, we're a bit late because I had an exam. She's my friend from Australia, and I brought her to experience a day in an Italian school. Can she stay for the class?"

The teacher shrugged and resumed explaining the finer points of Spanish grammar, not that the students were paying much attention. Occasionally some would look at the blackboard while the teacher explained verbs and sentence structures, and one or two may have taken some notes, but they quickly resumed their socialising. When the class ended, the teacher wrote the homework on the board and left. Hardly anyone copied it.

The next class was English and the students were being tested on their speaking skills. One by one, the students were called to the front of the classroom where the teacher proceeded to ask questions in English and the student attempted to answer, also in English.

I don't know how the students could focus on their exam, because their classmates were practically having a party. The teacher would occasionally turn around to tell them to keep the noise down but it made absolutely no difference. The party continued.

With my front row seat, I couldn't help but overhear every exam question and student's stuttered answer.

Lisa elbowed me and said in a low voice, "Don't stare. They're already nervous about the exam, and it doesn't help to have an English speaker in-class witnessing how badly they speak."

"Sorry, I didn't mean to," I whispered. "I was just surprised by how poorly they speak it. Especially the teacher! I thought they've been learning English for a few years already?"

"Yes, but it's not like the teacher is actually fluent in English or has lived in an English speaking country. She just learnt it from textbooks so it's broken English and that's what the students end up learning," Lisa explained.

I kept my eyes firmly on my travel diary for the rest of the class and only looked up briefly when it was Lisa's turn, to give her a thumbs up. She didn't need any luck. Her English skills and knowledge far surpassed the teacher's.

As soon as the bell rang, students from every classroom poured out into the courtyard and the noise levels rose to a deafening height.

"We have a five minute break," Lisa told me. "Let's get some fresh air."

"I need to use the bathroom."

"Me too. It's across the courtyard." She looked at me and grinned. "I'll give you a tour of the most famous students in my year level on the way."

"Huh?"

"You'll see."

The courtyard was a concrete square with nowhere to sit or anything pleasant to look at.

"Are they – are they smoking?!" I asked Lisa.

As though it was the most natural thing in the world, students everywhere were lighting up cigarettes. Teachers walked past without even glancing in their direction.

Lisa laughed. "Smoking is a national pastime here. Look over there. See that guy wearing sunglasses and talking on his mobile?"

I scanned the crowd and nodded when I spotted him. He was very Blingy.

"He's what we call a 'figetto'."

"A what?"

"It means someone who is overly obsessed with their looks. That guy will only wear brand name clothes, and he's been bragging for weeks that his belt cost €300."

My mouth dropped open. "€300 for a *belt*?"

"He's an only child so his parents buy him whatever he wants. And over there," she pointed in another direction, "see the couple making out? We call them Romeo and Juliet."

Completely oblivious of the crowded courtyard, the young couple were sucking the life out of each other. They seemed to be in the world of their own.

I looked at Lisa with raised eyebrows, a silent question for more details.

"They had a child together and it was put up for adoption because they're so young. Their parents put them in separate classes, but the teachers have given up trying to keep them apart. Every chance they get, they find each other. Everyone's sure they'll get married as soon as they are old enough."

"Wow," I breathed, amazed by the story and their ability to keep kissing without needing to resurface for air. "The Romeo and Juliet story doesn't seem so far-fetched from the truth now."

"Toilets," Lisa nodded her head to the unmarked door.

"Um, which ones are the girl's toilets?"

"They're unisex. Hurry though, our break is almost over. I'll meet you back outside."

She marched in and went into an unoccupied cubicle. I walked into a cubicle and froze, staring in horror at the floor. Instead of the toilets I was used to, these were the ones that you have to squat over. A hole in the ground with a slippery place for your feet on either side. My strongest childhood memory of these toilets was being afraid that I would slip and fall into the hole, or that I wouldn't be quick enough to get in and out before the boys climbed up to peak over the cubicle door. Not ideal facilities but I answered nature's call as quick as possible and escaped into the sunshine to wait for Lisa.

"Last class for the day and then we have the whole afternoon free," Lisa said, wiping her hands dry onto her pants.

"What is it?"

"Philosophy, and I should warn you about the Professor. He's a little… eccentric."

"How eccentric?"

"You'll see," was all she answered.

We resumed our seats at the front of the classroom and the rest of the students came in from their break. Except, it seemed that they intended to continue their socialising during class. Several minutes after the class had technically started, the Professor reluctantly dragged his feet to the teacher's desk. His longish brown hair was unbrushed, and he kept pushing up his glasses. His dark clothes seemed to match his mood.

No one paid any attention to him, not as he walked to the front of the classroom, or when he pulled out his books and began speaking. I looked around the classroom but none of the students were even looking in his direction. It was as though he was invisible. The Professor spoke to the air in front of him, his gaze not fixing on anyone or anything.

"Why is everyone ignoring him?" I asked Lisa in a quiet voice.

"No one likes philosophy. They think it's a useless subject

and he doesn't like students," she explained, flicking through her notebook.

The Professor slammed the notebook down on the table and muttered to no one in particular, "What's the point? I'm just wasting my time. It's not like anyone listens anyway."

Perhaps he sensed me staring because his head snapped in my direction.

His eyes widened and his muttering ceased.

"Have you always been in my class?" He asked, a hint of alarm in his voice.

The poor man thinks he's hallucinating.

"No, I'm an overseas student here for a visit," I stammered nervously.

I always get flustered when I'm placed on the spot in awkward social situations.

"She's with me, Professor," Lisa told him.

He looked at me for a moment longer, shrugged and resumed his lecture to no one.

I felt awful for him. It was incredibly rude of the students to completely ignore him like that, and it was clearly affecting him. No one likes to be made to feel invisible and insignificant. I did the only thing I could do in that situation, which was to give him my attention. I made sure I kept an interested look on my face as he rambled on about different philosophical theories which I couldn't understand or possibly hope to remember. Perhaps he realised, because as he left the end of the class he nodded his head in my direction. It was the saddest class I have ever attended and I was very glad that school was over for the day.

I didn't have time to think about the Professor's predicament for long. Lisa had a full afternoon of exploring planned for us, and I wanted to make the most of the short time I had left with my friend.

• • •

My time in Brescia was flying by, far more quickly than I liked. Every afternoon Lisa would take me somewhere fun and interesting, like the café' that served 32 different tastes of hot chocolate. Sometimes we even managed to convince Gabriel to take a break from studying and join us. The three of us went to visit the 'Falcon of Italy', a wonderfully preserved castle that sits at the top of Cidneo hill. It was free to go in and the beautiful gardens there had a spectacular view of Brescia. The history of the castle is interesting, and I should have paid more attention, but Lisa and I were more interested in having fun. After admiring the view of the city, the three of us turned our attention to the stone lion statues in the gardens. Well, to be perfectly honest, Lisa and I were the ones that came up with silly ideas and coerced Gabriel to go along. Just like when we were kids. Lisa and I thought it would be hilarious to take turns shoving our head into the lion's open mouth, while the other one pretended to be rescuing the victim about to be eaten. We could hear Gabriel sighing as he was forced to take photo after photo while we posed and sniggered.

Most evenings Lisa and I would take a stroll to the circolo to visit Kobi, then walk to other cafes' and meet up with Lisa's friends until it was time to sleep.

One night Lisa and I had volunteered to cook dinner so we walked to the local supermarket for ingredients. It was already dark and cold, we were hungry and the shopping bags were heavy.

"Let's take a shortcut home," Lisa suggested.

We turned down a dimly lit residential street, chatting about our plans for tomorrow when I sensed the presence of someone else. I glanced over my shoulder but the street was deserted. Besides me and Lisa, and a cat looking at us through a fence, there was no one else around.

It's just my overactive imagination, I told myself and kept walking, but I couldn't help feeling like we were being watched.

After a few metres, I couldn't ignore my growing sense of apprehension any more. Trying to act natural, I casually turned my head a little to look behind me, completely convinced I would see nothing. At first, I didn't see anything but a movement in the periphery of my vision caught my attention. I turned my head a little more.

A man wearing a long coat was walking behind us. The dim light hid his face but he looked to be in his thirties or early forties.

He's probably on his way home for dinner.

So why couldn't I shake off the feeling of unease?

We kept walking but my senses were on high alert. I could hear his footsteps now, and they seemed a lot closer. I turned my head to find the man was now *much* closer.

Don't panic, he could just be in a hurry to get home, I tried to convince myself.

"Noor? Did you hear me?"

"Huh? Oh sorry, I was distracted. Let's walk faster."

Lisa looked at me with surprise, then behind me at the man. She didn't say anything and looked calm, but stepped-up her pace.

"We need to turn here," Lisa said.

Oh good, I thought with relief. *We'll lose him now, just in case he was following us.*

I heard footsteps behind me.

This time, Lisa also turned around to look at him.

He had turned down the same street we had.

Coincidence? Perhaps.

Then again, what if it wasn't? I didn't like jumping to conclusions about the man that may or may not be following us, but after hearing enough news stories about assaults on young women, I had become suspicious of strangers.

"Lisa," I whispered nervously. "Is he following us?"

"I don't know," she said quietly and sped up.

So did he.

"What should we do?" I asked unsure.

Lisa practically shouted, "If anyone gets close to us, I'll hit him in the balls with this!" and began energetically swinging the large cabbage in her shopping bag.

I burst out laughing. While Lisa was swinging the lethal cabbage in the air, I turned to look at the man. I don't know if it was the swinging cabbage or the threat of violence towards his private parts, but the look of alarm on his face and the way he scurried to the other side of the street sent me over the edge into hysterical laughter. Lisa kept swinging the cabbage menacingly above her head until he was completely out of sight, and then started laughing.

Poor man. He was probably just on his way home to dinner when he was threatened with violence from a vegetable.

I learned two lessons that night:

1) If you are young woman out at night, don't take short-cuts down small streets and laneways. Even if you are with a friend, exercise great caution.

2) If you are in danger, vegetables can apparently make a handy self-defence weapon. Especially cabbages. Also, it helps to have a brave friend like Lisa.

It was my last day in Brecia and Lisa wanted to take me on a final excursion to Lago di Garda (Garda Lake). The only way to get there was by train, and the only way for us to get to the train station was our usual travelling method. By now I was an expert at sitting on the back of Lisa's bike and indicating to cars whenever we needed to turn. The weather wasn't ideal, cold and foggy, but that wasn't going to stop us from having one last adventure together.

The fog didn't lift. It was so dense we could barely see the lake.

"Wow, I've never seen it so empty here," Lisa commented. "It's busy in the tourist season."

"We must be the only ones crazy enough to come out in

this cold," I said, shivering under all the layers I was wearing. "Except for the pigeons and that guy with the clipboard. Petition?"

Lisa sighed. "Yeah, and I really can't be bothered dealing with petitions right now. Uffa! He's standing right in front of the way to get to the train station too." *(Ugh!)*

"Can't we go another way and avoid him?"

"No," Lisa grumbled. "Let's pretend we only speak English. If he thinks we're tourists, he'll leave us alone."

"Good idea," I agreed quietly. I didn't like giving out my name and details to strangers.

Plan in place, we walked towards him and tried to avoid eye contact but he wasn't having it.

Stepping right in front of us, he shoved his clipboard under our noses.

"Ciao. Could you stop a moment and sign this petition?"

"Sorry," Lisa said in English. "No Italian. We only speak English."

I tried not to blow our cover by giggling and stepped around him so we could leave.

"No problem," he answered cheerfully and stepped in front of us again. "I speak English very well."

My jaw dropped. Lisa and I looked at each other in surprise.

"Where are you from?" he asked us.

"Belgium," Lisa answered smoothly, having recovered her poise much quicker than me.

"Australia," I mumbled, still a little shocked at this unexpected turn of events.

"Really? My uncle lives in Sydney!" The man said excitedly. "He taught me English."

I tried to think of something to say and only came up with, "You speak it well."

"So, will you sign my petition?" He asked again.

Lisa asked him what it was about and he launched into a lengthy explanation while I hopped from foot to foot, trying to keep warm. Lisa signed and when the clipboard came my way I automatically signed, mumbled something like nice to meet you and made a hasty exit.

"What are the odds of him speaking English? Most Italians can't!" Lisa hissed as we walked away quickly towards the train station.

"I know! I can't believe his uncle lives in Sydney. What are the odds of *that*?!"

"I thought maybe the universe was punishing us for lying?" Lisa said with a laugh.

"Me too," I admitted. "I was so embarrassed! What was the petition about anyway? I couldn't focus on what he was saying."

"Animal rights," she said.

"Oh good," I said relieved. "At least it was for a good cause."

We spent the train ride home planning Lisa's visit to Pollone in the next few weeks, for one last adventure together before I returned to Australia. I refused to think about having to say goodbye.

CHAPTER 17
MONK + WOODEN CLOGS = FIERA DI DONNAS AND SANT' ORSO

Grandma and I settled back into our daily routine pretty quickly and my time in Brescia seemed a bit like a dream. I had gone from daily adventures to a very quiet existence on the slopes of the Alps, but I didn't mind. I loved reading by the fire and taking my daily walk to the lake in Parco Burcina.

At first she pretended she hadn't missed me and that it had been a relief to have her house back to its original tidy and peaceful state. I knew better than to believe her though because she kept calling me the Italian equivalent of *dear* and *love*. I even caught her humming while ironing my clothes AND she hadn't criticized my messy hair in days (I didn't bother brushing it every day. What was the point? It was just me and Grandma).

I watched her dip a biscuit in her milk and coffee.

"Admit it," I tried again. "You missed me while I was in Brescia."

"Nonsense. I could listen to the news without your loud music blaring from the next room," she answered without looking up.

"I know you missed me," I told her with a smirk.

She toyed with her cup and glanced up. "Hmpf. The house may have felt a little empty- " As though afraid she had revealed too much emotion she quickly added, "That's only because I got used to you barging in and out and leaving your things everywhere. And playing that music like we're at a disco!"

I laughed and gulped down the rest of my milk and honey. It was as close to an admission as I was likely to get.

"You better get ready, Gigi will be here to pick you up soon."

She had barely finished speaking when we heard car tires crunch the gravel outside. I quickly put on my boots, coat, scarf and gloves.

"I'll get you a present," I promised, double checking my wallet was in my bag.

"Don't run, you'll slip on the ice!" Grandma called out while I rushed out the door.

Shivering, I slid into the back seat and pulled the blanket over my legs.

"Ciao Gigi, Ciao Sara," I greeted them with more enthusiasm than I usually have so early in the day.

"Ready for the fair?" Sara asked with a smile.

It was freezing outside and not much warmer in the car but I didn't care. I had been waiting for this fair for weeks. My excited lasted for about 10 minutes before I fell asleep for the rest of the one hour car ride.

"Wake up," Gigi's voice jolted me back to reality. "We're here."

I rubbed my eyes and looked out of the window.

"Where are we exactly?"

"This is the village of Donnas. They have an annual wood-carving fair 10 days before the one of Sant' Orso," Sara explained.

"Oh." I looked at the street lined with pretty stone cottages. "I thought we were going to the one of Sant' Orso…"

"You and Gigi will," Sara assured me, "but this is a much nicer fair because it is smaller. Thousands of people go to the one at Sant' Orso and it gets so crowded you can't see anything."

Gigi locked the car and marched ahead, his big snow boots clearing a path for us in the slush. "Watch out, there's a bit of ice on the ground," he called out over his shoulder.

We turned into a long, narrow cobbled lane between a row of stone cottages with stalls in front of them. Each stall already had a crowd of admirers.

"I can't believe it's so busy already!" I said to Gigi and Sara.

Gigi grimaced. "This is nothing. By lunchtime you won't be able to move!"

"That's why we had to come so early," Sara explained.

"If you see something you like buy it or it will be sold before you can come back for it," Gigi added.

I had saved my Christmas money from Grandma and Amalia for this fair. I love wood carved ornaments and used to play with the ones my Grandpa had made, and Amalia's collection, every chance I got. Today I would be starting my own collection.

"How long have they been doing this fair?" I asked Sara.

"I'm not sure about Donnas, but I know that the fair of Sant' Orso has been going on for more than 1,000 years," she answered.

"You mean 100," I said.

"No, 1000. Actually, this year is its 1007th anniversary," Sara told me. "The fair has always been held between the 30th and 31 January, since 1000 a.c."

Stunned, I looked around. This was more than a fair. The artisans and the people at the fair were keeping alive a very old tradition for the next generation, and hopefully for many more. It was a privilege to be part of it.

"Do you know how it started?" I asked curiously.

"The story is that a monk who lived in Aosta used to carve

wooden shoes and hand them out to the poor during winter, to protect their feet from the snow. They say the fair is held in the same area where he would hand out the shoes, 'sabot' as they call them here," Sara explained. "When the monk died, people honored his memory with the fair but now it's more to show traditional craftsmanship."

"Everything here is hand carved in the traditional way," Gigi added.

Making the most of the apparently small early morning crowd, we took out time walking up. It was difficult not to linger at every stall but I wanted to see as much as I could before it became too crowded. Each stall displayed exquisite handmade objects, but some things were magnificent and drew a large crowd. My favourite was a replica of Fort Bard almost as big as me. The detail was incredible.

"Can I take some pictures?" I asked the craftsmen standing close by like a proud parent.

"Certo." *(Of course)*

"How long did it take you to carve this?" Gigi asked.

The craftsman laughed, a deep and robust laugh. "More than six months."

Wow. I couldn't imagine working on something for so long to get the detail so perfect.

"How much are you selling it for?" Sara asked.

"4000 euro, but it has already been bought. I'm only displaying it for the fair."

I gasped. With the current conversion rate that was almost $8000 AU, but I knew that if I had the money I would have definitely bought it. It was truly an exquisite piece of art.

"It's absolutely beautiful," Sara said as we moved on.

There was so much to see it was difficult to know where to look. We decided to walk up the lane looking at all the stalls on one side, then down again while looking at the stalls on the other side. My second favourite piece was an incredible, almost life-size Vespa motorcycle. Again, the detail was mind blowing. The craftsmen had lovingly carved every detail to be as realistic as possible. The asking price: €2000. If only I had won the lottery before coming here...

Not everything was out of my price range though. I bought roses made out of tree bark for Grandma and Amalia, and the traditional rooster and owl good luck charms for myself and my family. As big as my thumb, they were the perfect size for a tourist with an already full suitcase. There was still a lot more to see but all our stomachs were grumbling.

"Time for lunch," Gigi cheerfully announced. "We'll grab a quick bite and come back."

"You're in for a treat today," Sara told me. "I know you like trying local food so I thought we could have 'miasa'."

"What's that?"

"It's a flat polenta crêpe and you choose the filling. I recommend having it with the local cheese, Toma but it's also really good with sausage."

"Quick, before the line gets any longer," Gigi ushered us forward.

An elderly woman sat behind a very hot, flat cooking plate. Her arms didn't stop moving. As soon as she ladled the polenta mixture and smoothed it, she flipped the ones already cooked, stuffed and rolled them.

"Why don't we get some with Toma cheese and some with sausage?" Gigi suggested.

I nodded, my eyes fixed on the elderly woman. She moved with lightning speed and didn't burn a single miasa. The line moved forward quickly and in no time I was holding a couple of miasa wraps, one with Toma and one with sausage. They were warm, crunchy and mouthwateringly delicious.

"While we're here, I'll stop by the bakery and pick up the black bread," Sara told us.

"The one we had at the restaurant? Is it really black or is it just called that?"

Sara laughed. "It does look black but it's done on purpose.

For the fair they stuff it with figs, chestnuts and spices. Wait for me here, I'll be back soon."

When she returned, her arms were full. "I got you a loaf to share with your Grandma and Uncle, and some lard and honey so you can try it the traditional way."

"Thank you!"

I had never tasted lard before and I wasn't sure about drizzling it with honey but surprisingly, it went well with the black bread. We enjoyed some roasted chestnuts and vin brülê and waddled back to the fair.

Gigi and Sara had been right. Now that it was lunchtime we struggled to walk back down the lane for a second look at the stalls. It was so crowded that at a certain point where the lane narrowed, the crowd got stuck. Bodies pressed against each other trying to move forward, but it was a bit like being in a funnel with a blockage. I'm not the tallest person so I struggled to see over the bodies crowded in front of the stalls, and after being separated from Gigi and Sara a few times, they made me hold onto the backs of their jackets so I wouldn't get lost.

Somehow among all this chaos, the local band managed to march through the crowd. Ears throbbing from the loud music, I tried to flatten myself against the wall of a cottage, hoping I wouldn't fall to the ground where I would most likely be trampled.

We eventually made it back to the car in one piece, exhausted but very happy.

TEN DAYS later I was back in Aosta with Gigi for the Fiera di Sant' Orso. It was very similar to the one at Donnas, but on steroids. Many more stalls and hundreds more people. It was so crowded I struggled to get close enough to the stalls to see the beautiful craftwork, and it was so noisy my ears throbbed. Freezing and frazzled by the chaos, we left soon after lunch.

Even though I was glad to have seen the fair of Sant' Orso, the smaller fair at Donnas was definitely my favourite experience out of the two.

CHAPTER 18
SLEEPY SORDEVOLO

G randma's lips were pressed into a thin line. She bustled about the small room, putting things away a little more noisily than usual. I quietly placed my bag on the hard couch.

"What's with the oversized bag?" She demanded, critically eying it.

I ignored her comment about my medium-sized gym bag. "Is that why you're in a bad mood? Because I'm going to stay with Amalia?"

"I'm not in a bad mood," she snapped.

Supressing a sigh, I rubbed my forehead. "If you don't want me to go, I can talk to Amalia and just keep going for day visits as I've been doing."

I was really hoping it wouldn't come to this because I was looking forward to staying with Amalia and Enzo.

"You can't do that! We agreed you would stay with her for five days so you have to go, but when do *I* get to spend time with you? You travelled from the other side of the world and are spending time with everyone else except me!"

"What are you talking about? We're together all the time!"

"I've hardly seen you in the time you've been here," she

accused. "Day trips to Aosta, Turin, Biella, Brescia, Milan… " she listed, counting them on her thin fingers.

I drew a deep breath and didn't respond immediately. She'd become very irritable lately and often complained that I was getting home late from my day trips, even though I was almost always back in time for dinner.

"You're leaving soon and we've hardly spent time together. And – well … it's just that …"

"What?"

"I mean – I'm old and will probably die soon and never see you again!" she burst out.

Guilt hit me like a punch to the stomach. There was some truth in what she was saying, but what could I do? Everyone was making demands on my time and when I tried to refuse, Grandma accepted for me.

"Why didn't you tell me it bothered you?"

She shrugged her shoulders and shoved the cutlery in the drawer.

"I don't have to go anywhere," I tried to placate her. "I'll just tell people I'm busy."

"You can't do that! It would be rude to refuse their invitations."

"But – I mean - what else am I supposed to do?" I spluttered.

Grandma didn't respond and started re-folding the tea towels. Her head was down and she was avoiding eye contact, a sure sign that she was trying to hide her emotions.

I walked over and hugged her around the shoulders. "Let's make the most of my last few weeks here, ok? I won't go on any more trips so we can spend lots and lots of time together."

"But people will be offended! They'll think you don't want to see them!"

I shrugged. "I'll explain I want to spend the rest of my time with you. I'm sure they'll understand, and if they get offended - well that's their problem."

Grandma shook her head but didn't argue.

I hated seeing her upset and didn't want to leave like this.

"I saved for years just so I could see you again. I wanted to come back and spend time with you. You know that, right?"

Grandma nodded and patted me on the back. "You're a good girl. You kept your promise and made an old woman happy."

"And I'll come back again. I graduate uni in a few years and it will be easier to save when I have a proper job."

"Huh. I'll be dead by then."

"No you won't. I bet you'll still be chopping your own wood when I come back."

The corner of her lips twitched into the beginning of a smile.

"I suppose you had better head off now. Are you sure you don't want Enzo to pick you up from here?"

I shook my head and picked up my bag. "It's okay, I'll meet him at the post office. Besides, it's disgustingly warm and sunny for this time of year so I might as well get some exercise."

"Stop wishing for snow! You wouldn't have been able to go on so many trips if it had snowed all winter like you wanted."

"Yeah, yeah, I know." I looked at her and grinned. "I love you old woman, even though you nag me."

Grandma pretended to throw a tea towel at me. "Get out of here you little pest!"

Laughing, I waved and skipped out the door.

I LOVED WALKING through the village. No traffic jams or crowds of people rushing to and from work. If it wasn't for the tendrils of smoke billowing out of chimneys, I would have thought the village was deserted. Every now and then, someone walked by and said 'Buongiorno'. They were all well over their sixties. Many of the young people had moved to bigger towns and cities to study or work which left the village feeling a little like a retirement home.

I had just finished posting my letters when Enzo arrived. Amalia was waiting for us at home but we took a little detour to the cemetery so I could finally say goodbye to Great Aunt Denise.

Her twinkling blue eyes and kind smile looked down at me from the memorial photo.

"I wish I could have seen her one last time. Or at least come to the funeral," I said quietly.

"She loved you girls so much." Enzo dabbed his eyes with a large handkerchief.

I smiled at zia Denise's photo. "We loved her too. And we'll never forget her."

"Aaah," he sighed and blew his nose. "She looked forward to your weekly visits so much."

"I remember she used to stand by the window waiting for us to arrive… Do you know, me and Marina kept all the Kinder Egg toys she gave us."

"Ha! Yes, I remember that. She used to buy you an egg each every week."

Pretending to clean my glasses, I quickly wiped away the tears that were threatening to spill over. "We all miss her. Especially mum."

Enzo smiled. "When you're ready, we better head home. Amalia is waiting for you and we still need to stop by the bakery."

I lingered for a moment longer and followed him to the car in silence.

Grandma was right. This could be the last time I saw her, but it could also be my only chance to spend time with Amalia and Enzo. I didn't get a chance to say goodbye to zia Denise and I didn't want to have any more regrets. My limited time had to be shared and even though it wasn't ideal, it was better than nothing. Shoving the feelings of guilt to the back of my mind, I tried to focus on enjoying the present. Who knew when I would have another opportunity like this again?

BEEEEEEEP BEEEEEP BEEEEP.

Enzo loudly announced our presence on the narrow, windy road up the mountain slope to their house. It was impossible to see oncoming traffic around the bend.

My eyes darted to the side. If we got hit by another car, there was a good chance we would roll down the mountain. And there was hardly anyone around to help. A few run down looking mountain cottages dotted the slopes around us, close enough to see the smoke from their chimneys but far enough to be of no use in an emergency.

Whistling cheerfully, Enzo beeped again and turned the car onto the steep drive. Their double storey white house appeared into view and I spotted Amalia waving from the kitchen window. By the time we opened the front door, she was waiting at the top of the staircase.

"Did you have an accident? You were gone for so long - "

"No, don't worry, everything's fine," Enzo told her. "We stopped to visit my mum at the cemetery. You go upstairs Noor, I'll get some honey from my workroom and come up in a minute."

I had barely reached the landing when Amalia enveloped me in a hug.

"Finally it's my turn! I thought your Grandma might change her mind… "

"A deal is a deal," I told her with a smile.

"Oh, I've waited so many years for you to come back," she sniffed and wiped away the tears that had pooled in the corners of her eyes. "Do you think your sister will come back too? I want to see her again so much, at least one more time before I die –"

"You're not going to die for a long time," I told her firmly.

"And yes, she will come back to see you. She's already saving money."

"Ah, I can't wait to see her!" Amalia blew her nose and patted my cheek. "I'm so happy you're here. Only five days... well, let's make the most of it."

"I'm happy too," I said and hugged her.

"Come on, let's get you settled in. We prepared a bedroom for you," Amalia said, opening the door to the library/storage room. "It's one of those couches that turns into beds and I've put lots of blankets on. It's a bit small... "

I sat on the sofa bed and smiled at her. "It's cosy and comfortable, thank you."

The sofa bed took up most of the space and the corners of the room were crammed with large cow bells and a small bookshelf.

"Are those zia Denise's cow bells?"

"Yes," Enzo answered from the doorway. "After mum passed away, I brought them all here. Did I ever tell you that each bell has its own unique note? A good farmer knows his cow just by the sound of her bell."

Amalia sighed. "You can tell her about cow bells later. Let her settle in first."

I laughed. "Actually, I don't have much to unpack."

"Well, lunch won't be for a while. Is there anything you want to do?" Amalia asked.

"I can help cook."

"Nooo," Enzo jumped in. "You're on holiday, enjoy yourself. Go for a walk or something. There's a nice little waterfall and stream nearby."

"It's too cold to go for a walk," Amalia said. "What if she gets sick?"

"Nonsense, there's nothing better than mountain air!" He turned to me and smiled. "One of these afternoons I'll take you for a walk higher up the mountain."

"She's on holiday, not a hiking expedition!"

Chuckling, I put on my jacket. "I like walking, and I promise I won't stay out too long."

Enzo looked pleased but Amalia less so. She insisted I put on gloves, hat and wrap the scarf around my neck twice before she let me leave.

It was cold, but in an invigorating kind of way. I strolled toward the sound of running water and soon found the waterfall and stream. Mesmerized by the sound of water rushing over rocks, I lingered until I started shivering and my stomach grumbled. I was halfway back to the house when small flecks fell onto my glasses. Startled, I looked up and gasped.

"It's snowing! It's finally snowing!!" I yelled to no one.

Instead of rushing back home like I knew Amalia would want me to do, I danced a little happy jig right where I stood. The rest of the walk home was very slow, mostly because I kept stopping to try and catch snowflakes on my tongue or in my hand. Some more dancing may have occurred. By the time I made it back, Amalia and Enzo's worried faces were pressed against the upstairs window.

"What took you so long?" Enzo asked, taking my jacket.

"Did you get lost?" Amalia added.

"No, but it started snowing on the way back so I, um… stopped to look at it."

Amalia chuckled, shook her head. "I should have known. Come here –" she ushered me in front of the fire place, "- get warm while we set the table."

Lunch was delicious. Enzo was an excellent cook, and both he and Amalia kept trying to add more food onto my plate, which was hard to resist. The afternoon passed quietly and peacefully. Amalia sat in her favourite chair crocheting a very intricate and delicate ornamental curtain, looking up every few minutes to smile at me. I amused myself writing in my diary and answering letters from friends in Australia until Enzo surprised us with roasted chestnuts. When it was time to prepare dinner, I was ordered to sit in front of the fire place and rest. I read one of the books Uncle Francesco had lent me and after dinner, Enzo made everyone hot chocolate which we enjoyed in front of a roaring fire and a television show.

That was the only quiet afternoon I had for the rest of my stay. The mornings were more or less the same. Amalia would wake me up by kissing my forehead. After breakfast, I would walk to the waterfall then read or write until lunchtime and the afternoons were devoted to excursions or activities. We visited a small church so high up in the mountains that only the most devout would attend. We had our photos taken at a professional studio so Amalia and Enzo could have a souvenir of my visit. Amalia's hairdresser came to the house to give us makeovers which left me looking like a fluffy poodle. They ooohed and aaaahed and I hoped my cringe would pass for a smile. Questionable hairdo aside, the days flew by and my stay was splendid. Before I knew it, Enzo was dropping me off at Grandma's and in less than two weeks I would be flying back to Australia.

Saying goodbye was going to be hard. Especially because I didn't know how many years would pass before I could return, and if they would still be here.

CHAPTER 19
ANCESTRAL ROOTS

It seemed like only yesterday that I had arrived at the airport in Rome. Somehow, three months had passed and I was spending my last few days saying goodbye. Lisa had come to spend a day with me in Parco Burcina and I cried when she left. My cousins from Veneto had called to wish me a safe trip, and I spent some time with cousin Angela and her family.

Grandma and I made one last visit to the cemetery to say goodbye to Grandpa and his ancestors who are buried near him in the family crypt. I left flowers for them all, but there was one person in particular that I was deeply interested in – my great-great grandfather.

In 1859, before Italy was unified as one country, a baby boy was left at an orphanage in Piemonte. The practice at the time was for the priests in charge of the orphanages to give the children a first and last name, and they had a lot of fun doing it. Our family name is a wine preparation method. Other children were given types of cheese for a surname. I can only assume the priests were very fond of wine and cheese to name children after edible things.

When he was a young boy, great-great grandpa was taken in by a family in Pollone, but kept the name he was given by the priests. My mission was to investigate his origins and try to discover who his real parents were. Dad and I came up with a couple of theories, which perhaps were more amusing than realistic.

Theory 1: He was the illegitimate child of a serving maid and an aristocratic gentleman. Dad was very enthusiastic about this theory - potentially, we could be the descendants of royalty or nobility. It would explain Dad's expensive taste in wine and food.

Theory 2: He was the secret love child of a priest and a nun, which I thought was a more romantic origins story.

Either way, we were quite sure he was illegitimate because if he had been orphaned, his parents' relatives would have taken him in. Unless of course, they were all wiped out by some epidemic and he was the last survivor.

I had already checked the local council records and town archives in Biella with no luck, but the local church's parish records might have some information. Luckily for me, the elderly priest Don Pietro had agreed to let me look through them.

THE OLD CHURCH was as impressive as I remembered, but I had only ever been to the church hall and had some trouble finding the door to the residential quarters. When I found the green door Don Pietro had described, I knocked and knocked but no one answered. After several more minutes of waiting and knocking, I tried to enter through the church hall but the door was locked.

I looked at my watch and sighed. I'd been knocking for almost ten minutes.

No one's here, he must have forgotten.

Giving up, I walked down the church steps towards the road.

"Hello?" A frail voice called out.

Stopping abruptly, I spun around to look but couldn't see anyone.

"Hello?" The voice called out again. It was coming from the residential quarters.

"I'm here!" I yelled, running back towards the green door.

An old man with a head of sparse, thin white hair stood at the door.

"Sorry, I was checking the church door because no one answered …"

"Can I help you?"

"Um, I'm Noor. I have an appointment with Don Pietro to search the parish archives."

"Aaaah, si, si! I am Don Pietro. I'm sorry, my memory isn't what it used to be. You look familiar… Weren't you a little girl in my parish years ago? I haven't seen you at church in years."

"Oh, um… yes… living in Australia… " I mumbled, blushing.

I didn't mention that I had skipped having my first communion or that my church attendance was mostly 'absent'. If he didn't remember that, I wasn't about to remind him.

"Aaah yes, the family that moved to Australia. Come in, come in! I'm sorry to have kept you waiting. My hearing isn't so good and it takes me a while to get to the door from my rooms."

I could see why. The place was like a maze, one dark and musty corridor after another.

"No problem, I wasn't waiting long. And thank you so much for this opportunity," I added, following him closely.

There was no way I could find the front door again on my own, and the dark musty corridors were creeping me out.

"Almost there. I keep all the parish records in my rooms towards the back. You can take as long as you want and go through them all."

"Thank you, I really appreciate your tim -"

BANG!

Gasping, I jumped away from the closed door next to me.

Vicious snarling ripped through the air.

The door trembled with the force of each thud.

"Giuglio, it's only me and a friend," Don Marco said very calmly.

"What is - I mean, who is Giuglio?" I stammered.

"Oh, don't mind him, he just gets a bit grumpy when I have visitors."

THUMP!

The door shook with the force of Giuglio's body smashing against it.

He took turns between snarling and barking and trying to smash his way through the door.

Probably to lunge at my jugular.

Don Pietro shuffled past the door calmly, with me scuttling close behind, heart banging against my rib cage.

"In here," Don Mario waved me through the door.

The small room was slightly less musty than the rest of the house. Shuffling to a large cupboard against the back wall, Don Pietro opened it and started rifling through thick files.

Giuglio continued calling for my blood. His howls and snarls echoed loudly down the corridor, sending ice down my spine.

"What century were you looking for?"

"Oh, um… 1859," I answered, half expecting Giuglio to appear.

Don Pietro put a large pile of folders on the table.

"Here you go, these are all the records I have of that time. Take your time going through them and call me if you need anything."

"Wait, what? Where are you going?"

Don Pietro raised his white eyebrows. "I am going to finish my work."

"But - but - you're leaving? I mean, Giuglio sounds very angry… "

Laughing, Don Mario waved a chubby hand as he walked to the door.

"Just ignore him, he is locked in the room," he called over his shoulder.

Drawing a deep breath which did not calm my nerves, I sat down and started going through the files. I knew the names of my ancestors, where and what year they had been born so it narrowed down my search a lot. I flicked through the old yellow papers as quickly as I could without damaging them. I must admit, they were impressive records. Written in beautiful neat scroll handwriting, each person belonging to the local parish had an entry with their details and those of their parents. Several entries had 'Born during Napoleon's reign' written in beautiful handwriting.

Giuglio's incessant snarling and thumping against the door kept me focused on the task at hand. If he kept this up, the poor doggie was going to make himself sick with stress.

Please be here, please be here, I silently begged, searching for my ancestor's name.

Yes! I found him!

Carefully pulling out the paper, I double checked the details to make sure I had the right person. Same date of birth, same location of birth and death, same details of spouse and children. It was really him. I read it carefully, looking for the information I really wanted and had risked being mauled to death for - the name of his parents.

Orphan.

I read the entry again, double checking every detail, every word in every line.

Orphan was the only word written next to Parents.

My heart sank. All this searching, all this trouble and I was no closer to discovering our origins than I had been when I started. The details of his parents were either unknown, or deliberately not filled in. Sighing, I carefully put away the documents and moved to the door.

"Don Pietro, I finished."

He must have been close by because this time he arrived within a couple of minutes.

"Already? That was quick."

"Yes. Thank you so much for letting me search through the records."

"Did you find what you were looking for?"

"Not quite. I think I may have to give up …"

"That's a shame, but at least you tried. Unfortunately that's the way things were back then. Many babies were given to orphanages for many reasons and the parents' names weren't usually recorded. So, tell me about Australia. Is it true you have kangaroos in your gardens?"

I laughed and broke the sad news to him – no, we did not have kangaroos wandering around in our backyards. He was curious about life in Australia, so I chatted to him for a few minutes before walking back to Grandma's house.

I hadn't discovered what I really wanted to know, but on the other hand my research had not eliminated the possibility that my ancestor was the illegitimate son of nobility. Possibly even royalty. Or more amusingly, the secret love child of a passionate and forbidden liaison between a priest and a nun. How many people can say that about their origins? Maybe it was a good thing we didn't know. It didn't really matter anyway. I knew that every generation since great-great grandpa had been bred, born and buried in this sleepy mountain village. My ancestry tied me to this place and while I had family living in Italy and Australia, I was in a very privileged position to call both countries home. As for me, I knew without a doubt that the mountains would always feel like home, in whatever country I ended up in.

CHAPTER 20
ARRIVEDERCI

"I'm going out for a bit," Grandma said, heading for the door.

I finished wrestling my jumper into the suitcase and looked up. "Where are you going?"

"I told you I have an appointment today. Don't you listen?"

"Sorry, I forgot. What's the appointment for? Are you sick? Are you going to the doctor?"

"You ask too many questions," she replied, buttoning her coat. "And no, I'm not going to the doctor. You just focus on packing your suitcase and I'll be back soon."

She was out of the door like a lightning flash, leaving me with an impossible task.

I'll have to leave my clothes behind so the gifts can fit, I thought.

I cringed, picturing Mum's face when she found out I had left perfectly good clothes behind. Then I pictured Grandma's face if I left behind any gifts from her, my Uncle, my cousins and dad's friends. Either way, someone was going to get annoyed with me. With a deep sigh, I pulled out all my clothes except for the ones I was going to wear tomorrow and put the rest in a pile on the couch. Grandma could donate them to a charity here, although knowing her, she would probably keep them for my next visit. Even with all the clothes out, it took me almost an hour of re-arranging things to make everything fit.

I had just finished packing and was adding a log to the fire when the door opened and Grandma walked in, gently patting her hair. Her neatly brushed, fluffy, white hair was had been replaced by carefully arranged curls.

"Wow nonna, I don't think I've ever seen you look so glamorous before." I closed the front opening of the wood fire stove and stood up. "What's the special occasion?"

"It's for tomorrow."

"Why? What's happening tomorrow?"

"Tsk, tsk. Have you forgotten you're leaving tomorrow?"

"No, but what does that have to do with your hair?"

"I have to look presentable at the airport. What would people in a big city like Milan think if I went dressed as I usually am?"

I stared at her for a moment, too stunned to reply straightaway.

"But - I mean, you've never gone to the airport because you don't like busy crowds …"

"Who knows when I'll see you again?" She said, not quite meeting my eyes.

Am I seeing things or are her eyes a little moist?

Blinking back tears, I crossed the small room and hugged her.

"I love you Grandma," I said softly, hugging her tighter.

Patting my back in the comforting way she used to when I was a child, she answered just as softly. "You've made me so happy. If I die soon, I'm glad I got to see you one last time."

I was in danger of being overwhelmed by my emotions. How would I get through tonight and tomorrow? How do you say goodbye to someone, not knowing when you can see them again and fearing they could die in the meantime? Grandma was 84 years old. Yes, she was healthy and more active than most young people I knew but I couldn't pretend she was young anymore. I couldn't take for granted that she would live many more years.

It was all worth it for these weeks together, I thought. *All the long hours, rude shoppers, working on weekends and school holidays, not buying things or going out much so I could save... It was all worth it.*

Grandma smiled at me and patted my hair. "I hope you finished packing because just about everyone will be stopping bye tonight to say goodbye," she informed me.

I frowned, half annoyed at the lost time with grandma and half grateful for the distraction. Left to my own devices, I might have spent the night crying.

The rest of the night, like the other two before it, was simply chaotic. Angela and Amalia cried as they clutched me to them, while I tried to comfort them without crying. It was a lost battle. Luisa and Gigi led a steady stream of Dad's friends who brought a few last minute gifts that I had to try and fit in my luggage. In the end, I gave up and shoved them in the pockets of my pants and coat. Those that couldn't make it in person called. By the time everyone left I was emotionally drained and physically exhausted, but I couldn't sleep. I was dreading tomorrow.

FOR THE FIRST time since I arrived to the sleepy village of Burcina, I woke up before Grandma. By the time she had come downstairs I was dressed and my bags were by the front door. She looked as drained as I felt.

We had breakfast together one last time, in silence. Neither of us could bring ourselves to talk and when Uncle Francesco arrived he found a miserable pair. I put on the winter jacket he had given me at Christmas and headed to the door.

"Wait," Grandma held onto my arm. "Come here a minute."

With an intense look of concentration, she tugged and fiddled with the pocket on my jacket. I raised my eyebrows at Uncle Francesco. Looking slightly amused, he shrugged and continued loading my luggage into the car.

"What are you doing? What did you put in there?" I moved to slip my hand into the pocket but she smacked it away.

"Don't touch it!" she ordered. "Flying is dangerous but this will keep you safe."

"Hurry up," Uncle Francesco called. "The traffic will be bad, we have to leave *now*."

I paused at the front door for one last look, trying to memorize what the house looked like before rushing to the car. I kept my face pressed against the cold window, staring at everything as we drove through the village.

I'll come back, I promised myself.

It was a very quiet one hour car ride. At some point I remembered Grandma putting something in my pocket so I pulled it inside out to look. The serene face of the Black Madonna stared up at me, securely attached to my jacket with a safety pin. Swallowing the lump in my throat, I removed the safety pin in case it beeped as I passed through airport security, and carefully placed the Madonna icon in the travel pouch hidden under my jumper. It would be safe with my passport and close to me during the long flight.

THE CHECK-IN WENT SMOOTHLY and I stayed with Grandma and Uncle Francesco until the last possible moment. She had never been to an airport and was fascinated by the arrival and departure of planes. The take-off was exciting, but she would gasp and watch anxiously every plane that was landing. I spent most of the time reassuring her that it was very safe and comfortable, and you barely noticed the take-off and landing inside the plane.

"7am Flight to Melbourne is now boarding," a smooth voice announced over the PA system.

"It's time," Uncle Francesco said.

Grandma had given up trying not to cry and the tears slid down to rest in the wrinkles of her cheeks. "This could be the last time I see you," she half whispered.

I hugged her and didn't want to let go.

I better make this quick so she doesn't see me cry.

The last thing I wanted to do was upset her even more.

I pulled away and plastered a big smile on my face.

"I'll be back. It will take me a while, but I *will* come back to see you."

"I might be dead by then," she pointed out.

"You better not be," I threatened in mock anger.

"You won't be dead," Uncle Francesco argued. "You're in better shape than me!"

"When they made you, they built you to last," I teased.

Grandma scoffed but didn't argue.

"I'm not going to say goodbye," I told her and Uncle Francesco. "You never know what the future will bring so I will just say 'arrivederci'." *(Until we meet again)*

Uncle Francesco leaned in to hug me. "Have a safe flight. Be careful."

"I will," I promised.

I looked at Grandma, trying to memorize her face before I gave her one last hug.

"Stay alive so I can come back to see you," I whispered.

"I'll try," she promised. "I hope I can see your sister too, just one more time."

We let go, reluctantly, and I walked away looking over my shoulder and waving until they were out of sight. Only then did I stop holding back my tears and let them flow.

Would I see her again? Or Amalia or Angela and my cousins? I really hoped so, and whatever happened in the future, I would always be grateful for the time and happy memories I had shared with them.

I walked to the boarding gate with tears running down my face, but my heart was beating faster in excitement. Soon I would see Mum, Dad, Marina and my little fur-ball Susu. It was a very bitter sweet moment.

DEAR READER

Thank you for reading!

If you liked this book, have a look at my other travel memoirs. They can be read on their own and in any order, and they are available as ebooks and paperback. If you prefer to read in chronological order, here is my suggestion

Big Cities and Mountain Villages

Falafels and Bedouins

Christmas Lights and Carnevale

If you have a minute, please consider leaving a review on your favorite social media platform. Readers trust other readers, and reviews are the lifeblood for writers.

Enjoy photos of my travels at

https://www.facebook.com/NoorDeOlinad/

Made in United States
North Haven, CT
15 December 2022

29011399R00126